Surviving and Succeeding in Large Law Firms

While Keeping Your Honor and Dignity

Paul C. McCoy

Book and ebook design by Booknook.biz

Elite Legal Publishing, Inc.
EliteLegalPublishing@gmail.com

ISBN 978-0-578-92678-0

CONTENTS

1

How to maximize the benefit of this book.

If you seek insights on how to have a successful career at a large law firm, you are holding the right book.

I am keeping this book short so that you can read it more than once. Each Chapter is dedicated to a very specific topic, so that you can use it as a resource time and again as new issues and challenges present themselves during your career. Here are the five situations in which you should read this book:

1. Read this book before law school to give yourself a feel for the profession you are joining.
2. Read this book during law school before you choose a law firm to join. I recommend reading it during the summer between your first year of law school and your second year of law school.
3. Read this book again before you start working at the law firm you have chosen. I recommend reading it after you have taken the Bar Exam, but before you start work, because that is a rare period of calm when you will not be studying or working, but you will be hungry for the knowledge in this book as you await the start of your career as a lawyer.

4. Read this book again, once during each of your first five years of practicing law. You will be amazed by how the advice in this book takes on new meaning as you gain experience.
5. Read any particular Chapter of this book at any time you hit an issue for which the advice in this book might help. This book is best used as a resource guide over time.

It is also important that you only implement the aspects of this book that resonate with your personality. Authenticity is critical. If you try to force yourself to be somebody you are not, the façade will collapse under pressure. Perhaps you will find in this book advice that you immediately understand and implement, and perhaps other aspects of this book will make more sense to you over time, in which case you will be able to implement the latter advice as and when it resonates authentically with you.

2

Why do you want to be a lawyer? And, why do you want to be a lawyer in a law firm?

Why do you want to be a lawyer?

It is critical that you ask yourself this question and give yourself an honest answer. You would be surprised by the number of students in law school who have no good answer to this question. Such lack of clarity does not bode well for their futures as lawyers. There is a good chance that if you do not have a clear reason for becoming a lawyer, you will either (i) drop out of law school, (ii) leave the practice of law early in your career even if you finish law school, or (iii) choose the wrong area of law to practice after law school, making your journey to success much more arduous.

This book is focused on surviving and succeeding in law firms. There are many paths for law school graduates, and joining a law firm is just one. Many new law school graduates go to work for the government. Many go to work for corporations. Many go to work for charities, universities, NGOs, civil rights organizations or private foundations. Some simply start their own law practice, either alone or with other new law school graduates. The list of careers for new law school graduates goes on and on, but this book is focused on surviving and succeeding in a law firm, and so we must ask the next question …

Why do you want to be a lawyer in a law firm?

If your answer is that becoming a lawyer and joining a law firm is second nature, because one or both of your parents were lawyers in law firms, then you are in luck. Over the course of my career, I saw many Junior Associates join law firms for precisely this reason and it worked out fine. The amount of information such young people acquire during their childhoods about the realities of being a lawyer in a law firm, simply by having been reared by lawyers, is substantial. But of course, such people are a small fraction of the total number of people who seek out careers in law firms.

If your parents were not lawyers in law firms, as mine were not, the life of being a lawyer in a law firm is probably a mystery to you, as it was for me. If so, it is important for you to really understand why you want to be a lawyer in a law firm. The three reasons that seem to carry people the farthest in a law firm are: Money. Prestige. Challenge.

Money

There is nothing inherently wrong with wanting to make money. Cultures seem to be all over the map on this topic, however. Some cultures see making money as glorious and some cultures see it as an evil necessity that shouldn't be discussed openly. In my view, money is the lubricant that keeps the machinery of life moving. Without it, everything grinds to a halt. This is true at the macro level of national and global economies, and it is also true at the micro level of individual lives. In the United States, there are only two professions in which admitting that your primary desire is to make money is viewed by some as unseemly—medicine and law. There is a misconception in our country that being motivated by money will somehow undermine your integrity as a lawyer. This fallacy makes it very hard to admit to yourself and others that making money is a primary reason for wanting to become a lawyer and join a law firm. If it is your primary reason, do not fret. I assure you that being motivated by money and having integrity in your representation of Clients can be completely harmonious.

Discussing money can be awkward, but let us state openly that compensation at large law firms is much higher than the salaries paid in other professions to individuals with similar levels of experience. One of the greatest rewards for me of having substantial disposable income is the ability to give generously, sometimes to a friend or family member in a tight spot, but every year to charities. My two favorite charities are The Food Bank and Music in Schools Today (aka MuST). Being able to contribute to these organizations makes me feel more successful than any traditional measure of success. I hope you find charities that resonate for you, I hope you give generously during your career and I hope you experience the same sense of reward from being able to do so as I have.

Prestige

Prestige is another key driver for people who are ultimately successful in law firms. Hollywood may portray lawyers in a negative light, but the reality is that becoming a lawyer is prestigious. It requires a college degree and then a law degree and then you must pass the Bar Exam. The difficulty alone makes becoming a lawyer prestigious. But it is also prestigious because lawyers are the guardians of the fabric of civilized society—i.e., law. Lawyers bring laws to life in our advice, advocacy and negotiations. Very few roles in society are as prestigious as facilitating the implementation of law into society. Becoming a lawyer is prestigious, and practicing law in a large law firm is, in my view, the most prestigious of all careers for a practicing lawyer.

There is a unique confluence of factors in large law firms that vest prestige in the successful large law firm lawyer. First of all, the practice of law in any law firm, large or small, is the central activity, the *raison d'etre* of the organization, which is very different than the peripheral role for lawyers in government (other than criminal justice), practicing law in corporations, practicing law at non-profit organizations, and so on. In a law firm, all of the resources and energy are focused on the practice of law. At other organizations, because the overriding purpose is something other than the practice of law, the resources and energy given to the practice of law suffer by comparison. Second, there is intense competition to obtain a position at a large law firm and thereafter ongoing competition to survive and succeed at a large law firm. Such competition weeds out many; those who survive are exceptionally talented and dedicated, genuinely deserving of prestige.

I enjoyed the prestige that came with my career at my law firm. I had a corner office at One Market in San Francisco, which is one of the best offices any lawyer in any law firm in the world could possibly want. My views extended out over the San Francisco Bay in one direction and over the city of San Francisco the other direction. Business trips brought me frequently to cities around the world, including London, Zurich, Dubai and Singapore, as well as all over the United States from Seattle to New York City and many places in between. I was called upon by some of the world's most intelligent and ambitious thinkers, such as the leadership at the Bill and Melinda Gates Foundation, The Lumina Foundation for Education, University Hospitals Health System, Harrington Discovery Institute, Credit Suisse, JP Morgan, Nuveen, Franklin Templeton, Goldman Sachs, Morgan Stanley, CalPERS and CalSTRS. I interacted with genuine power-brokers in a world that grew more and more intertwined with private investment activity, which was my area of expertise. Ultimately, I was recognized in California, nationally and globally by three leading independent arbiters of legal talent: *Super Lawyers, The Legal 500* and *Chambers and Partners.*

Challenge

The challenge of practicing law in a law firm is surpassed by no other career. If you seek a multifaceted challenge, and if choosing to become a lawyer and choosing to join a law firm are driven by your desire for challenge, then you have an extremely good chance of being very successful practicing law in a law firm.

I used the words "multifaceted challenge" above, because practicing law at a law firm is not simply a matter of knowing the law. Sure, knowing the law is challenging. But in fact, knowing the law is the easy part. It is an open-book test, so to speak. You can always look up the law when needed. The real challenge of practicing law in a law firm is the enormous juggling act. Many times, during my career I found myself representing dozens of Clients simultaneously on dozens of different cases, interfacing with dozens of opposing lawyers who represented the adverse parties, all while coordinating with my colleagues to staff such matters within my law firm and interface with regulators or other third parties germane to the successful outcome of the cases. Over time, I also took on firm leadership responsibilities as the Practice Area Leader, globally, of the Private Equity Funds Practice Area at Morgan Lewis. When you toss all of this in the air and begin to juggle, it is an incredible challenge, believe me! If you are seeking a career of inexhaustible challenge, joining a law firm will satisfy you *ad infinitum.*

Justice. Equality. Fairness.

What about justice? What about equality? Fairness? Aren't these the grand principals of law and shouldn't they be the core motivation for any decent person who desires to be a lawyer? Yes, of course. Take me for example. I was completely enamored by the Age of Enlightenment and the stroke of jurisprudential genius that gave birth to our Constitution. When I got to law school, I consumed every law class I took with relish; never tiring of the pursuit of justice displayed in case after case studied. Justice, equality and fairness are so fundamental to law that I take it for granted that nearly all lawyers have a moral compass tethered to justice, equality and fairness at the beginning of their careers. Sadly, some stray from such noble beginnings. But even though some stray, the vast majority of lawyers I dealt with during my career remained rooted in principles of justice, equality and fairness. Contrary to the way in which popular entertainment portrays lawyers, I have found them to have a much greater sense of integrity than the general public and among the very highest levels of integrity of all professions. I believe this is because lawyers, for the most part, are grounded in justice, equality and fairness. (It is also true that it is enormously detrimental to one's career if one becomes known as untrustworthy. See Chapter 27 *Never Lie. Never Blame.*)

While nearly all law students care deeply about justice, equality and fairness, the fact remains that the lawyers who survive and succeed at law firms usually have one of the three *additional* motivations discussed in this Chapter: A desire for money, prestige or challenge. The perfect candidate desires all of the above.

3

Full disclosure about practicing law at a law firm.

In many areas of law, there is a requirement that a party to a business transaction provide full disclosure to the other party of all material facts necessary to prevent one party from misleading the other. It is a basic premise in all anti-fraud statutes. Given that there are such disclosure requirements throughout law, it has always amazed me that there is no effort to provide young people full disclosure about becoming a lawyer before they enter law school or before they join a law firm.

Here is a piece of my story, and I hope it provides some disclosure to those considering a career practicing law with a law firm.

From 1993-1995, I was a Financial Program Specialist in the Financial Management Service within the U.S. Department of the Treasury. It was an interesting job. I focused primarily on banking relationships between the U.S. Treasury and banks around the world to ensure our agencies operating around the world had the correct amount of local currencies at the right time and place to conduct their businesses. So, for example, if the Department of State needed Rupiah in Indonesia, I would set up a banking relationship in Jakarta, Indonesia to enable currency exchange from Dollars to Rupiahs (and back again as necessary). In this job, I interacted with banks in dozens of countries and I made a reasonable salary for my age. I held the job from 22-25 years old.

In 1994, while I was still at the Treasury Department, I attended a party in Washington, D.C. The crowd was a mix of young professionals, college students and grad students. At some point in the evening a young man announced that he had been accepted to law school. I saw a flicker in the eyes of nearly every girl at that party. With each congratulations, their voices had new admiration and adoration for the young man. He had elevated socially right before my eyes. He was clearly more desirable after his announcement than he had been before, and I knew in that instant I wanted to go to law school. I had toyed with the idea before. I even discussed it with my undergraduate business law professor. He shared with me some of the realities of being a lawyer and successfully dissuaded me. I remained dissuaded until that party in Washington D.C.

Fast forward to the fall of 1998, when I joined Linklaters in their London office (Linklaters is an English law firm) as a first-year Associate. A typical day for me at Linklaters began at 6:00 a.m. I awoke and, if I had not already been dreaming about the cases piled on my desk, my first thought upon waking was to check emails and voicemails about such cases. Always there were many new emails and voicemails, because Linklaters was a global law firm and our Clients were located around the world. While I slept, Clients and colleagues in other time zones were working and sending me emails and leaving me voicemails. A flash of dread would pulse through me every morning upon seeing the volume of emails and voicemails.

I felt a special pang if there was an email from a Partner. I would read the email and invariably find a mixture of criticisms and demands, but with an oddly friendly tone. The criticisms were typically couched as tips for how to do better next time whatever I had most recently done, and the demands were typically two or three new tasks that must get done "asap." You will learn to hate "asap" and "urgent" and you will find yourself chuckling a loathsome chuckle at "emergency"—really, no one is dying, nothing is on fire, just what is the "emergency?" The criticisms sting the most, because whatever tips for improving the Partner sends, she seems to have no appreciation for the fact that you were up until 2:00 a.m. trying to perfect work that is, in hindsight, so unbearably imperfect.

You will note that I said the Partner's email of criticisms and demands had an oddly friendly tone. This was a psychological nuance that caught me completely by surprise. My background did not prepare me for this at all. My father was in the army. There were only two kinds of messages: positive messages in a friendly tone and negative messages in an unfriendly tone (to say the least). One could write a PhD thesis in psychology analyzing the many reasons why Partners at law firms use a friendly tone even when delivering unfriendly messages, but be warned, it makes the messages dig into your brain in a most unpleasant and confusing way.

After scrolling through to determine which emails, if any, needed immediate responses and after providing such responses, I would get ready for work and make my way via the Underground to One Silk Street, London. I usually arrived by 9:00 a.m., which sounds cushy until you realized I left every night between midnight and … well some nights not at all (the so-called "all-nighter"). By noon each day it was clear that there was no way I would complete the new tasks before midnight, again staying late. I would try to recall the last time I went home at a reasonable hour, or perhaps even went out to dinner with friends, but then would realize such line of thinking was counterproductive. I would force myself to stay in the present, which as it turned out was an endless flow of work and work-related feedback circling feverishly for 13-16 frenetic hours every business day.

Weekends, glorious weekends! I would typically have only six or seven hours of work to get done over a weekend and was otherwise able to go out and about and have fun. I was very young and even the 70-80-hour work weeks did not exhaust me enough to keep me from having some fun on the weekends. And for the first time in my life, I had enough money to have a proper good time.

Note that when I interviewed with Linklaters, as is the case for any law student interviewing at any law firm, I was told about the incredibly sophisticated legal work being done there, as if truly it was the very most interesting legal work in the world; the likes of which I couldn't possibly hope to find at any other firm. In hindsight it amazes me that anyone would describe endless hours of legal research, writing, proofreading and countless menial tasks as "the very most interesting legal work in the world." Law firms have a tendency not to disclose that the high-profile cases and huge transactions, which are at a macro level very interesting, are not at all interesting at the level of fine points and critical details being run to ground by a Junior Associate. A Junior Associate lives at the intersection of tedious and critical. The need to find all relevant precedent, for example, is tedious; but because the case is high profile or the transaction is huge it is critical that you do not make any mistake … at all … not even a typo.

There is good news, which I must include in my disclosure. If your primary motivator for joining a law firm is money, prestige or challenge you will receive it; in fact, you will receive them all. See Chapter 2 *Why do you want to be a lawyer? And why do you want to be a lawyer in a law firm?* And, truthfully, I am not aware of any profession in which someone can become as successful as law firm lawyers without a similar relentless dedication to their work. As such, this Chapter is not meant to discourage anyone from pursuing a career in law, but rather to calibrate your expectations about what a career in law looks like in the early years.

4

A law career is neither a sprint nor a marathon; it's thousands of sprints.

Many reading this book will have had an experience similar to my law school orientation experience. There I was, young and excited to be joining an elite club—future lawyers. In my mind, I could already see the enormous contributions I would make to justice while simultaneously earning enough money for a mansion and sports cars. It was pretty much perfect in my mind.

The orientation was held in a large auditorium with traditional theater style seating for the audience and a stage for the speakers. I do not recall much from the orientation other than one concept that our Dean emphasized. I had never heard it before, although I must say I have heard it many, many times since. He said, "law school is not a sprint, it is a marathon." He went on to explain that unlike a sprint, wherein you use all of your energy in a short burst of activity, a marathon requires skillful pacing of your energy and endurance. A marathon is a long, arduous task and requires a steady long-term mindset. Law school, according to our Dean, was the long arduous pursuit of legal knowledge and skills.

Upon joining my first law firm after law school, the orientation speech the Chairman gave was similar. The Chairman used the same analogy, stating that the practice of law was not a sprint, but rather a marathon. He emphasized the importance of not burning out with a burst of energy at the beginning of one's career, but rather he encouraged developing stamina for a long, arduous—albeit rewarding—career.

Having successfully completed law school, taken (and passed) the Bar Exam in New York and California, and having practiced law from the 1990s until 2020, I can tell you this: Practicing law is neither a sprint nor a marathon. Practicing law in a law firm is, in fact, a series of one thousand and one sprints with brief periods of rest from time to time. Practicing law is similar to final exams in law school, but the intense period of "finals" never ends, it becomes your new norm until you have mastered your area of practice. That is the cold hard truth.

Why do I make this point? I think it is important because the marathon analogy is flawed. It is, I agree, better to think of your career as a marathon than a single sprint, for sure. It would be awful to start you career with a burst of energy and several months later realize that you were completely burned out, have a nervous breakdown and quit. So, we all agree it is not a single sprint. But is it really a marathon? Is it realistic to believe that with your training and the establishment of a healthy sustainable pace of working eight hours per day five days per week you will succeed in the practice of law? Absolutely not. It's just not accurate. There will be periods of intense frenetic activity that do not allow for reasonable pacing of your efforts and there will be occasional slow periods during which you can rest. In essence, a law career is analogous to a series of many, many sprints. At times it will feel like you are running multiple different sprints simultaneously; some of the sprints are ending while others are in progress and still other new sprints are starting.

Unfortunately, there is not enough discussion in law school about the nature of the workload for lawyers. Every law student seems to have a vague understanding that lawyers at law firms work long hours, but very few law students could describe the true nature of the workload over a typical year at a law firm.

I remember interviewing a law student for an open position at my law firm.

Me:	Do you understand the demands of our workload as lawyers?
Candidate:	Yes, I read on AboveTheLaw.com that Associates at your law firm are expected to bill 2,000 hours per year.
Me:	And that is fine for you?
Candidate:	Well, yes, why not?

She seemed almost confused by my questioning. I could see into her mind. She had already calculated that 2,000 hours divided by 52 weeks is only 38.5 hours a week. She likely had even done the math with vacations factored in—i.e., 42 billable hours per week over 48 working weeks in a year. Behind her smiling eyes, she was thinking, "They are going to pay me all that money to work 42 hours a week! Law school was the best decision of my life!"

Me:	What about vacations?
Candidate:	Oh. Well, I think if I bill 42 hours a week, I could take four weeks of vacation.

And there it was, what I suspected. Her view of a billable hour was like a widget one could make at any time and, even better, one could moderate the number of widgets one decided to make on any given day during any given week. My heart sank; not just because she clearly did not understand the nature of practicing law, but also because I had the unenviable task of being the one to explain it to her. So, I continued, asking a few more questions.

Me: How much time have you factored in for non-billable tasks throughout a typical day?

Candidate: [Blank stare.]

Me: Well, most people estimate about an hour of non-billable time for every three billable hours. This is a reasonable assumption while you are an Associate. The ratio only gets worse after you become a Partner and have many more responsibilities beyond doing billable work.

I could see her mind racing to calculate new results on a per week basis. I decided to help her out.

Me: If you have 2,000 billable hours in a year it means about 2,667 total hours of work. If you divide that by 48 weeks—we must save four weeks of vacation for you—that means 55.56 hours per week on average.

Candidate: [Color returned to her face.] That's no problem.

Me: You need to know that work ebbs and flows in the practice of law.

Candidate: Okay.

Her eyes didn't even flicker; the notion of ebb and flow meant nothing to her in this conversation—it was too abstract.

Me: So, that means if you have one slow week out of every quarter it must be made up during the other weeks.

I saw the racing calculations begin, again. I helped, again.

Me: It means that 2,667 hours of work is really done during the course of 44 weeks, not 48, and that's if we continue to assume you take four weeks of vacation.

Candidate: Okay.

Me: Well, that's 60 hours a week or more during your busy weeks.

Candidate: Okay.

But I wasn't done yet. There were two more facts about the workload in the profession of law that I needed to explain. How I wished these things were discussed in depth at law schools, so that newly minted lawyers would know what they were getting themselves into and so that I wouldn't have to be the one to tell them.

Me: Even during the periods when work is flowing, it is uneven. You may have weeks of 80 hours of work or more and weeks of ten hours of work, or less.

Candidate: Okay.

Now it was time for me to drop the bomb, and I had no joy in dropping this bomb as it was a bomb that blew up during my own vacations over the years.

Me: We cannot prevent work from flowing heavily at precisely the time when you might have a vacation planned.

I had gone too far. I could tell she was thinking that either I or my law firm was outrageous in these expectations and that surely another law firm would be more reasonable. So, I added the only beneficial facts that are truthful.

Me: We have a large team and we try to cover for each other. And technology allows us to go on our vacations even when workflow peaks, it just means you develop skills at getting work done remotely. Overall, if you understand that work can build up during the year to require very long hours and even intrude on your vacations, that's what I'm really trying to confirm. It's best if we both feel comfortable that you know what you are agreeing to get yourself into here.

She liked this very much. In her mind I had circled back to what she vaguely understood even before the interview, which is to say that working at a large law firm requires working long hours.

I very much liked the relief I saw in her expression. In my mind I felt better knowing I could hire a talented, intelligent, motivated new lawyer and with any luck she had a little more understanding of what would be expected of her.

We (the law firm) made her a job offer. She accepted.

5

THE BEST BUSINESS ADVICE I EVER RECEIVED.

I want to share with you the best business advice that I have ever received. It is important to understand that practicing law in a law firm is just as much about building a business as it is about providing legal advice and services to Clients. The following quote from Maya Angelou is the best business advice I have ever received:

> *"People rarely remember what you say; they sometimes remember what you do; but they always remember how you made them feel."*

The amount of energy lawyers spend making sure they are always correct in what they say and always correct in what they do is impressive. It is critical, too, because the practice of law is at its core giving the correct answer and doing the correct thing, always. Who wants a lawyer unable to give the correct answer to a legal question or unable to develop winning litigation strategies? But so many—an astonishing portion in fact—never focus on how they are making others feel.

Your Clients have emotions. It may not always seem like it, but they do. You might do the most amazing legal work in the world, but if you ignore your Client's feelings along the way they are not going to remember you fondly. If they do not remember you fondly, they will not send you more legal work of their own and they definitely will not refer you to others. If you have been condescending, dismissive, arrogant, or even outright confrontational with your Client, you are very unlikely to have a loyal Client. You are very unlikely to have built any trust with the Client. Put very simply, the Client will not like you. People hire people they like whenever possible.

Law firm Partners have emotions. Secretaries have emotions. Associates have emotions. File clerks, I.T. professionals, mailroom staff, all have emotions. There is no group of people, indeed there is no person, with whom you will interact to whom Maya Angelou's advice does not apply.

I remember a friend telling me she would never go on a second date with anyone who was rude to a waiter. She said it was a red flag about the character of the person. In a way, I believe this is Maya's advice at work. My friend was able to empathize with the waiter, and it made her feel bad to see the waiter being treated rudely. She would remember only that negative feeling about the date and there would be no next date.

If law firm Partners think you are a jerk, your career will suffer. That is obvious. But what might not be obvious is that your career will be hindered if secretaries, Associates, IT professionals, mailroom staff or anyone else contributing to the overall functioning of a law firm thinks you are a jerk. It is possible to succeed as a lawyer, even if you ignore the feelings of others, but you will have made it much, much more difficult for yourself; you will have made it much, much more difficult for those around you; and you will have diminished the quality of the law firm itself in the process. You will have even diminished yourself.

Keep in mind that how you treat others is a direct reflection of your own character. You are building your reputation with every interaction. No one is able to escape this fact. If you leave someone with bad feelings about you, that person does not go into stasis until the next time you interact. That person is out and about talking to people. You can be sure that when your name comes up, that person is going to speak up. In fact, people are far more likely to tell a friend or colleague about a bad experience or interaction than a good one.

I am not recommending being fake or phony. I am suggesting that there is no need to be anything but kind and courteous in your dealings in a law firm. It was not fake for me to befriend anyone at any position in the law firms where I worked. This was equally true when I was a first year Associate, a midlevel Associate and a Partner. I treated all with dignity, because all have dignity.

I was particularly sensitive to the need for leaving others with a good memory about how I made them feel, because I know that everyone suffers at some point in life. During the course of any given day, you are certain to interact with someone (usually more than one person) who is suffering in some respect. It could be physical pain. It could be emotional pain. It could be work overwhelm. It could be a dying family member. It could be a rocky love relationship or, more specifically, a divorce. It could be a neurological disorder such as depression, anxiety, vertigo, hypochondria. Perhaps most pervasive are feelings of loneliness or feelings of inadequacy. So, as I walked the halls of my law firm and as I interacted on the phone or by email with all different kinds of people, the one thing I always kept in mind in each situation was that the other person has emotions and is likely suffering in some way—that is the nature of life. Knowing that others are suffering, I would ask myself what simple thing could I say or do that would brighten their day even if only in a very tiny, tiny aspect? A kind word. A kind gesture. A compliment. Offering to help when it was not requested or expected. And if there was nothing

I could do, perhaps I could just listen. There are a million ways in which you can be a net positive to those you impact, rather than a net negative. And the best part, truly, is that it is extraordinarily rewarding to have had a positive impact. I suspect it is some sort of evolutionary phenomenon for the benefit of the species, but there is no doubt that being a positive force in the life of others rejuvenates and invigorates oneself.

I will share an example with you. I recall representing a public pension plan in connection with a very large investment transaction (approximately $1 billion). The investment related to companies in the life sciences industry, such as medical discoveries. The business professional leading the transaction at my Client had several degrees, including an advanced degree in science, a medical degree and an MBA. She was very proud of her degrees and was particularly proud of her status as a scientist. As with all large transactions, there came a point when things were not going well. The two sides—my Client and the other side—were not able to reach agreement on certain critical points in the contract. When speaking just among her team and me, out of the presence of the other side, she launched into a tirade about how illogical lawyers are; she made no distinction between me and the lawyers representing the other side. She didn't want to admit to herself that the business team on the other side of the transaction was digging in for better terms. She preferred to blame the turbulence on the lawyers—all lawyers. Of course, I took offense to this because it was clear to me the lawyers on the other side were simply following the instructions and wishes of their Client, just as I was simply following the instructions and wishes of my Client. Several clever retorts crossed my mind, each of which would have highlighted the absurdity of her tirade, but the words of Maya Angelou came to me. "They will always remember how you made them feel." So, I decided to move forward with the conversation, ignoring her tirade, and offered up several ideas for how to make compromises with the other side. Because I could see she was suffering under the stress of the transaction, I also went out of my way to remind her of all of the great outcomes the transaction would have, given her knowledge as a scientist. It worked. Her mood shifted immediately for the better and her focus also shifted to the various ideas for moving forward, rather than wallowing in frustration and lashing out at lawyers.

I handled many transactions for this Client afterwards, and I feel confident that had I taken the low road and unleashed a counter-tirade, I would never have had any further business from such Client. Furthermore, I am confident that if I hadn't recognized that the Client was suffering under the stress of the transaction and gone out of my way to ease that suffering, the Client would have continued to be insulting and unpleasant. Implementing Maya's advice led to a good relationship with a Client who had many large transactions in the pipeline for me, and this was just one of many, many times that Maya's advice served me well.

6

You must understand the relative value of your time to the time of others.

Below is a conversation that repeated in some version on many occasions. I would call a Junior Associate and leave a voicemail. I was busy and needed to move to another matter so I would leave a precise voicemail on what I needed the Junior Associate to do. Nearly every Junior Associate made the same mistake once (and usually only once): they would see that I had called and they would call me back. The conversation would go something like this …

Junior Associate: "Hi Paul. I see that you called."

Me: "Great. What's the answer?"

Junior Associate: "Um … well … I am not sure what you are asking."

Me: "You didn't listen to my voicemail, did you?"

Junior Associate: "No. Should I? I wanted to get back to you as fast as possible."

Me: "Yes, please always listen to my voicemails before you call me back. Only call me back if you have questions after considering carefully the voicemail itself. I think you will find I said everything you need to know to proceed and it is not a good use of my time to repeat it all again. It's also disrupting my train of thought on other matters."

Junior Associate: "Oh, I see. Okay, sorry."

The best Associates understood my point before this little conversation ended. Others didn't. If it happened a second time, I would then be blunt and ask them whether they thought their time or my time was more valuable. If they paused at this question, usually a reflection of their exaggerated sense of self-importance, I would state as a matter of fact that our hourly billable rates were substantially different. My time was empirically more valuable than theirs. I would also use the occasion to explain the same is true vis-à-vis Clients, because they are paying us (not the other way around). Nearly always, this lengthier explanation made it clear that it is never appropriate to return a phone call from a more senior colleague or from a Client without first listening to their voicemail.

This applies doubly so to emails. On occasion I would receive a phone call from a Junior Associate who had received an email from me, but had not yet read it. On occasion, the Junior Associate would say he was calling precisely because it was easier for him to talk to me than analyzing the email itself—"couldn't we just discuss it?" "Yes, of course," I would say, "after you have made an effort to proceed without my help." Again, I would explain the relative value of our time and that I had many other items that needed my attention. Struggling with the problem was good for him, of course, because it is the best way to learn and even if he could only resolve 50% of the overall task, that reduced by 50% what he and I would talk about when we did sit down to discuss the project. The 50% he had learned would inevitably make the remaining 50% easier to explain and open up natural pathways to discuss the next stage of the project.

I cannot list every scenario in which the relative value of your time to others is critical, but here are some of the most common:

1. *Problem Solving Part I.* A tough issue has come up on a case, and you believe the Partner could tell you the answer off the top of the Partner's head. It is important to think through (i.e., carefully analyze) the problem and try to solve the issue on your own using the vast resources of your firm before going to the Partner. Only when you have exhausted your efforts—see No. 3 below—is it appropriate to reach out to the Partner. You will then be armed with all the things you tried, which itself will save the Partner time. Your interaction with the Partner will become collaborative, as you describe what you have done already and she considers additional avenues to solve the problem. In fact, one of the clear distinctions between a Junior Associate and a Mid-Level Associate is the shift from mechanical to-do lists, which are used to guide Junior Associates, to collaborative interactions with Partners and Clients enjoyed by Mid-Level Associates.

2. *Problem Solving Part II.* Whenever possible, bring one or more proposed solutions when you bring a problem to a Partner. This is similar to No. 1, above, but it is worth emphasizing and differentiating. You may be under incredible time pressure and exhausting all efforts to find a solution may take more time than you have. You will always have time, however, to prepare a well

organize list of ideas you have for finding the solution before you go into the Partner's office. The Partner may say you are exactly on track, thank you for checking in, or the Partner may have a better approach. But what you should avoid at all costs is walking into a Partners office blank-faced, like a deer in the headlights, sputtering a problem and having given no thought how to solve it. Note that the degree to which an Associate was able to articulate a problem let me know if the Associate had made any efforts to solve it.

3. *Problem Solving Part III.* Exercise good judgment to know when you have exhausted your efforts to solve the problem without Partner input. This means applying your skills to the task at hand without cutting corners, but does not mean trying to apply your skills to a task that you do not understand. It is almost always a lack of understanding what is expected of you, a lack of understanding the task at hand, that results in wasteful efforts to accomplish the task. This is known commonly as "spinning your wheels." Exhausting your efforts, as stated in No. 1 above, could occur very soon after receiving an assignment, if after genuine efforts you simply don't understand the assignment. When this happens, organize your thoughts so that you have a clear set of questions about the assignment and go back to the Partner and get the answers you need.

It is equally annoying to a Partner for you to spin your wheels as it is for you to rush into her office seeking help prematurely. Spinning your wheels wastes time as the clock ticks towards an impending deadline, which makes the Partner's life more stressful. Also, spinning your wheels can run up billable hours that have to be written off rather than billed to a Client, which hurts a Partner's realization ratio within the firm (keep in mind that Partners are monitored and their performances measured in many ways in large law firms).

4. *Prepare for All Conference Calls & Meetings*. There are many times during the first few years of your career when you will be invited to a conference call or to attend a meeting, but you will not be leading the call or meeting. A common mistake of Junior Associates is to simply dial into the call or show up for the meeting and wait for the action to unfold like a play being performed for their entertainment. Fail! At the very least, you must review the materials that will be discussed and plan to take copious notes with as much precision as possible. That is the value you are expected to add and the reason you have been asked to join the call or meeting. But there is much more value you can add.

Partners have many, many things going on at once and they can lose their place during a discussion—for example they might forget an important detail or not recognize an unfair characterization of facts by others on the call. If an Associate is well prepared and is able to politely remind the Partner of the overlooked detail or call out the mischaracterized facts, that Associate will have made the Partner a lifelong loyal supporter. As one Partner friend of mine puts it, "Make me look good and you'll always have my support, but make me look bad and I'll fire you." To this day, I am a lifelong supporter of certain Associates who saved me during complex conference calls. Unfortunately, I can also remember those Associates who let me twist in the wind because they were either unprepared to help or too afraid to help. This harkens back to the advice in Chapter 5, in which I quote Maya Angelou, "*they will always remember how you made them feel*." A Partner does not enjoy twisting in the wind before important Clients, counterparties or opposing counsel, while an Associate sits silently unhelpful.

5. *Answer the Real Question.* Always answer the question behind the question. What is the question behind the question? Well, it is the information a Client or Partner needs to proceed even if they failed to state it in their initial question. Consider the following example:

Client: "I'm presenting on a panel at Great Businesses Conference; that's fine, right?"

This question is impossible to answer without knowing the context in which it is being asked. Clearly, the Client is protected by the 1st Amendment to the Constitution. She has freedom of speech and assembly and surely can present on a panel at a conference. But the question comes from the CEO of a startup company. Your firm is currently representing that company as they sell their stock privately to investors. It is, therefore, likely that the question behind the question is, "*Under the securities laws, is it okay for me to talk about my company to a room full of strangers and maybe even convince them to buy stock in my company?*" Well, now that we focus on the question behind the question, we see that there is an entire body of law implicated beyond the simple 1st Amendment question. The question behind the question is in fact a securities law question about permissible communications during a private company's efforts to sell stock. It is illegal to make a public offer to sell stock without having first registered the offering with the SEC. Speaking at a conference is generally considered a public communication, and offers to sell securities made while speaking at a conference is likely to be deemed by the SEC as a public offering of the security. The question behind the question requires you to be ready to provide securities law advice. If you had simply answered the surface level question, saying to the Client that of course they have the freedom of speech to speak at a conference, rather than answering the question behind the question, not only might your Client have engaged in a prohibited public offer of securities, but at a minimum you would have wasted their time by answering a question they weren't really asking. You would have looked foolish giving an answer rooted in the 1st Amendment and most likely lost the Client's confidence and future work.

6. *Ask Good Questions.* Know exactly what you need from a Client before getting on the phone with them to discuss their matter. The only way to get what you need from a Client, to do what you need to do for the Client, is to ask good questions. And the only way to ask good questions is to prepare.

Consider this situation: Ms. Partner, a Partner at your law firm, emails you and asks you to help with a Cease-and-Desist letter for Client X. Ms. Partner includes contact information for Ms. Bright, an internal lawyer at Client X and instructs you to reach out to Ms. Bright to help with the letter. Ms. Partner does not include any other information in the email.

Your first instinct might be to walk over to the Partner's office and try to get some context for her email and clearer instructions on what you should do. But you have read this book and you want to try and solve this situation on your own before going back to the Partner. You know that Ms. Partner's time is more valuable than yours.

Your second instinct is to pick up the phone and call Ms. Bright and say, "Ms. Partner asked me to help with a Cease-and-Desist letter; what do want me to do?" But you have read this book and you realize that your Client's time is more valuable than yours, too.

Surely, there is some way to develop good questions before calling Ms. Bright without interrupting Ms. Partner. You then google Client X and see that they are an apparel brand. You learn what you can about Client X from the Internet. You also know that Nice Guy, one of the Senior Associates, has been working a lot for Ms. Partner, so you ask Nice Guy if he knows anything about Client X. He does! He has been working with Ms. Partner and Client X for almost a year as one competitor after another tries to use logos, trademarks, tradenames and all manner of tricks to confuse consumers into buying their goods instead of Client X's. Nice Guy explains that the first step in fighting off these encroaching companies is to send a Cease-and-Desist letter. Nice Guy has done it a dozen times. He even knows Ms. Bright. Nice Guy warns you that Ms. Bright is very busy and she does not hesitate to bark at anyone wasting her time.

Based on the information you received from Nice Guy, you look up on your law firm's system some of the recent examples of Cease-and-Desist letters that your law firm has prepared for Client X. After only an hour or two you have a good sense of the framework these letters all seem to have in common. You organize your thoughts and prepare some good questions for Ms. Bright. You call Ms. Bright, introduce yourself and say you work for Ms. Partner. You immediately explain that Ms. Partner asked you to help with the new Cease and Desist letter and you ask your good questions: "Is this Cease-and-Desist letter going to be along the same lines as others we have done for you, recently?" "What is the name of the offending company and precisely what are they doing that must stop?" "Has Client X had any other dealings with the offending company?" You explain your familiarity with the other recent Cease and Desist letters your law firm has done for Client X and ask, "Are there any particular facts or issues that should be emphasized in this Cease-and-Desist letter as compared to the others?" "Are there any specific ways it should differ in approach from those our law firm has done for you recently?" You listen carefully to Ms. Bright's answers and take accurate notes throughout the call.

You hang up the phone and feel really good. The call went well. You can tell from Ms. Bright's tone that she was pleased by the fact that you had familiarized yourself with her company and the recent work your firm has done for her before you called. Ms. Bright hangs up the phone on her end with a good feeling about you.

7

Teach yourself; It takes the pain out of practicing law.

One of my mentors told me early in my career that whenever I receive an assignment the first thing I should do is go to the library (now everything is online of course), grab a treatise that covers the relevant area of law and read it. In other words, he was telling me that now that I no longer had professors to teach me, it was time to teach myself going forward. At first, I was so eager to do the assignments that were given to me that I ignored this advice. I would struggle to comprehend the nature of projects, how my tasks fit into the larger projects and why my assignments were an important part of the overall projects. Eventually, I came to realize how ineffective this made me and also how much it robbed me of any job satisfaction. How could I feel any sense of reward if my tasks were done without any understanding of how they fit into a larger project? We lawyers are curious and analytical by nature, so doing random assignments without any context is excruciating.

Perhaps an example will make my point. I was working on a securitization (a.k.a. repackaging) of $250 million of assets in 1998 for our Client, JP Morgan. A securitization is when a bank puts a bundle of individual assets into a newly-formed company and then sells securities in the newly-formed company to buyers in the market. The securities are usually debt securities and the project is often referred to as a "debt arrangement." JP Morgan had a small army of its employees working on the debt arrangement. JP Morgan also hired an accounting firm to assist with certain aspects of the debt arrangement. The accounting firm had a half dozen people working on it. Several other banks were involved to help sell the debt securities, and each of those banks had teams of people involved. JP Morgan hired my law firm, and we had eight lawyers working on the debt arrangement. In total, there were probably as many as 50 people involved in this debt arrangement in one way or another. Maybe more.

Two key documents are relevant for a debt arrangement. First, there is a Bond Indenture. It is more than two hundred pages long and sets forth all of the terms and conditions of the debt arrangement. Second, there are Notes, which are specific pieces of the overall debt and each Note is issued under the Bond Indenture. Basically, the Notes are a very short summary of the most important terms, such as the specific amount of the total debt arrangement that will be owed to the particular investor holding such Note, the interest rate applicable to such debt and the maturity date for repayment of such debt. The Notes are only three or four pages long.

I had two roles on the project: I was to read and reread *ad nauseum* the 200+ page Bond Indenture, scouring for typos, inconsistencies and errors; I was also responsible for preparing the Notes to match any changes in the Bond Indenture. This was done fairly easily because a sample of the Notes was one of the schedules to the Bond Indenture.

I didn't bother to read any treatise or other secondary source on securitizations (repackaging) of assets or debt arrangements. I simply assumed I would figure it out along the way. Clearly, my first responsibility to scour the Bond Indenture was reduced to simple proof reading for spelling and grammar, because I had no idea of the substance of what I was reading. Imagine the drudgery of reading and re-reading more than 200 pages of gibberish late into the night. My second responsibility—to keep the Notes updated—was easier, or so I thought, because all I had to do was update the sample Note in the Bond Indenture schedules every time there was a change in the Bond Indenture. I didn't need to understand why I was making such change, so long as they matched.

Every day the Junior Partner on the project would ask me, "are the Notes ready?" Every day I would answer, "Yes." I was a little confused why he kept asking, but I didn't ask him any probing questions to find out. I certainly did not know enough about how to succeed in the practice of law to ask him what the question was behind his question. (See Chapter 6, No. 5 *Answer the Real Question*).

After weeks of work, and many very late nights (some of which simply rolled into the next workday), we were nearly complete with the Bond Indenture. It was the evening before the Notes were to be evaluated by the ratings agencies, a critical step before selling the Notes to the market. Again, I was asked if the Notes were ready. Again, I said yes. But this time, my yes was a little shaky because I had grown less and less comfortable that the sample Note in the Bond Indenture was in fact the Notes the Partner was asking about. The Partner asked to see the Notes. I showed him the Bond Indenture and the updated sample Note in the schedules. The color drained from the Partner's face. He looked genuinely terror-struck. The sample Note was not at all what the Partner had been asking about. What the Partner had assumed I was doing was preparing actual final versions of all of the Notes to be sold to investors, each as a separate document and each including specific dollar amounts, interest rates and maturity dates based on a spreadsheet of data JP Morgan had provided to us. It turns out that the rating agencies want to see the actual Notes that will be sold, completed with all relevant information, and not simply the Bond Indenture and a sample Note.

We had 12 hours—from 10 p.m. to 10 a.m.—to prepare a slew of Notes with all of the final information included. Thankfully, with the help of the Junior Partner and two other Associates we were able to divide up the workload and complete all of the Notes by the 10 a.m. deadline for submission to the ratings agency. It was a very unpleasant all-nighter for me, and not because I had to work all night. Imagine the glares from time to time sent my way from the Junior Partner and the other Associates as the hours passed from late evening to midnight, then from midnight to the wee hours, and from the wee hours into the next morning. Perhaps the most intense glaring from the Junior Partner occurred as the office rumbled back to life in the morning, full of fresh, rested faces.

It took me months to redeem myself in that Partner's eyes.

If I had only read a treatise on Bond Indentures and Notes I would have had a much better understanding of what was going on in the securitization (repackaging) project. Understanding the components of selling Notes, the difference between a Bond Indenture and a Note and so forth would have made all the difference. I would have understood what the Junior Partner was asking me all along. I would have understood the project as a whole, making it less tedious because I would understand how my tasks fit into the project. I could have added more value, which is critical to getting any sense of reward from a job. And, importantly, the near-disaster with the ratings agency would never have happened.

So, I recommend that you teach yourself as much as you can about the area of law you are practicing in order to understand the greater context of your assignments, regardless of how narrow your specific assignments might be. Doing so takes a lot of pain out of the practice of law. If the example above was difficult to follow, because of the complexity of the subject matter, it makes my point even more. Every area of law is difficult at first and only digging in to study it makes it easier.

8

Train others; The benefits are exponential.

I often joked in the office that I liked training people, because once I trained someone how to do something, I never had to do it again, myself. But the truth is there are many extraordinary benefits to training others, beyond my jocular refrain. I discuss a few of these benefits, below. But first, I want to note that it is far more challenging to train others than most people realize.

The reason it is so difficult to train others is that the practice of law moves very fast. The number of emails and phone calls, alone, are enough to fill up each day. And most of those phone calls and emails must be answered in a short timeframe. And you must also research legal issues and draft documents. Taking all of this together, you begin to see why lawyers work twelve hours a day (sometimes more). Adding another hour here and there to train someone is painful; the additional time is on top of the already long hours of any given day.

But the time limits alone are not the only obstacle to bringing yourself to train others. In fact, although the days will remain fast-paced, by the time you know enough to train others, some pressure will have been reduced in your daily life. Partners and Clients will ask you to do things, and you will finally know how to do them. There will be a period of months, maybe even a year or two, when you are able to do what you are asked within the time that you are allotted without too much difficulty. By comparison to your earliest years, this phase of your career will feel easy and you will find that your energy reserves begin to rebuild. This phenomenon results because people are slow to change their perception of you, even while you are learning and changing. If they began working with you as a brand-new lawyer, when you are a fourth-year Associate they will not have fully internalized the fact that you have more than three years of experience. You are likely to continue to receive Junior Associate assignments, albeit with a mix of some more advanced assignments. There is considerable temptation at this point in your career to relax your efforts. After all, nobody notices because of the hectic pace of their own respective days. You can cruise along for a while doing tasks that have become easy for you.

Beware. Many lawyers who reach this stage in their career and elect to cruise along, instead of seeking further growth in their practice, ultimately leave law firms before making Partner. The lawyers who are dedicated to making Partner use the opportunity to develop in several critical ways, including training other, less-experienced lawyers.

When you make the effort to train others, you are building your own career. If you rely exclusively on yourself to handle work, there is a finite maximum that you can handle. That maximum workload also means a maximum revenue generation; this is particularly true in the field of law where most revenue is generated by hourly fees. If you train others to help you, you can become responsible for more and more workload, thus more and more revenue generation for the law firm. Think of yourself as a piece in the law firm's overall pyramid. When you reach the stage of your career when you are able to train others, you are probably no longer at the bottom of the pyramid, but you are not very far up the pyramid, either. Most lawyers have forty-year careers, give or take, and so if you are a 4th year Associate you are about 10% up the pyramid. Now, consider yourself the apex of a mini-pyramid you are building below yourself, tucked within the overall law firm pyramid. As you train others, your mini-pyramid becomes bigger. As your mini-pyramid becomes bigger, you become more and more important to the overall firm pyramid.

And there are other benefits, too, beyond expanding the amount of revenue you are responsible for generating. Training others will free you up from certain tasks that have become boring and will allow you to focus on more interesting tasks. This generates growth in your skills as a lawyer, as well as job satisfaction.

Training others builds loyalty. In fact, I can think of no better way to build loyalty than to train someone. After all, you are giving them assignments and you are teaching them how to accomplish those assignments properly. Teaching another person skills that will forever enable them to make a living, to support themselves and their families, and to pursue their ambitions both in and out of the office engenders tremendous gratitude. Gratitude is at the heart of genuine loyalty.

Training others increases your own authority in the office. Psychologically, the person being trained will always view you as their boss. Training others gives you implied authority, which grows as you train more and more people.

Now, let's consider the two paths that can be taken. One person decides to cruise for a while. We will call him Mr. Cruise. The other person decides to train younger lawyers. We will call her Ms. Strong. Over time, people at the law firm will begin to notice the difference between the activity surrounding Ms. Strong's office as compared to Mr. Cruise's office. Many more people will be coming and going to Ms. Strong's office, and loads more work will be getting done under her supervision. Office conversations will include reference to her, because she *and her team* are getting so much done. And I want to emphasize that they will refer to her as having a team! In fact, her team will speak of her often. This will multiply the positive reputational impact of the increased capacity of her work. In addition to increased quantity, having a team will allow her to take on more complex aspects of projects because she will have bandwidth to continue to teach herself (See Chapter 7 *Teach yourself; It takes the pain out of practicing law*). Taking on such increased tasks will further reinforce Ms. Strong's positive reputation. The Partners she works for will love her, because they are getting the benefits of Ms. Strong's expanded team. Those Partners will have greater freedom to focus on business development to expand their own practices. Ms. Strong is clearly teed up well to make Partner, because she has a team under her, she is growing her skills as a lawyer, she has a strong positive reputation and she is enabling the existing Partners to expand their respective businesses.

On the other hand, Mr. Cruise, who has decided to enjoy the period of relative ease as a Mid-Level Associate rather than take on the challenge of training others, will by the time he is a Senior Associate be more or less viewed the same as he ever was. He will not have a team growing under him, he will not be growing new skills as a lawyer, his reputation will not change and he will not be enabling Partners to expand their respective businesses. At best, he will be viewed as useful, like any static asset in an office. Mr. Cruise will not be referred to very often in office conversations because no one is working for him. The nature of his ongoing work will remain unchanged and unremarkable. He will be viewed by Partners as acceptable, but nothing special. His peers most likely will have the same professional opinion of him as the Partners. Eventually, Mr. Cruise will realize that promotion to Partner is unlikely and he will leave the law firm.

I should note, however, that every now and then there is a Mr. Cruise who does not leave the law firm. Sometimes they snap into action, eventually, and although they are behind the likes of Ms. Strong, the Mr. Cruise types can claw their way to promotion to Partner a year or two after Ms. Strong. Another possibility is that some stay cruising at their law firm indefinitely, for as long as they are productive and profitable to the law firm. But my focus in this book is not to discuss the many alternative and circuitous career paths for lawyers. My focus is to share with you the best ways to survive and succeed in a law firm, and one way, for all the reasons set forth in this Chapter, is to train others as and when you have the skills and opportunity.

9

Seek the most complicated assignments.

Seeking the most complex assignments will accelerate your career, create job security and enhance your enjoyment of being a lawyer.

Imagine you are sitting in a conference room with five Partners and ten Associates. The meeting is a weekly meeting to discuss the status of existing projects and to determine who should work on new projects. A Partner introduces a new project he landed, and he describes it as novel and extraordinarily complex. The Partner knows in his mind it will be difficult to get volunteers, but he seeks volunteers in any event, hoping to avoid forcing an Associate to work on the project. It is an unpleasant moment, because the Partner already predicts there will be no volunteers and he knows that whoever he picks for the project will feel they have been unlucky to receive the assignment. The Associate chosen may also wonder if being chosen is a sign she is unliked, because she is forced to take the unwanted assignment. When the Partner does ultimately assign the project, the Partner feels bad and the Associate feels unlucky and perhaps unliked.

But what if you raised your hand and volunteered? What if you recognized that the only thing bad about the project is the daunting task of navigating something new and complex? You might realize that nearly everything you are asked to handle is new to you and dauntingly complex from your perspective. This new assignment is no different. Even the most complex assignments, as perceived from a Partner's perspective, are really no different than all other assignments, as perceived from your perspective.

Think of it this way: Just because a project is perceived by a Partner as being novel and complex, it does not mean the project is somehow more novel to you than other projects; it also does not mean that the project is more complex than other assignments in an absolute sense. It means only that the project is new territory for the Partner and, because the Partner has never done such a project, he perceives the project as novel and unusually complex.

You must resist the podium effect when partners describe new assignments as novel and complex. The podium effect is the phenomenon in society that whoever is speaking from a position of authority—historically, from a podium—such person must be right. Because of the podium effect, when a Partner perceives a project as novel and complex it sends chills down the spines of the Associates.

But you are in luck. You have read this book. You know that it is quite likely that the Partner does not face new territory as often as a Junior Associate like you. Nearly all tasks are new territory for Junior Associates. Nearly all tasks are complex for Junior Associates. Most tasks during the first few years of practicing law are novel and perceived as complex from the perspective of Junior Associates. You realize this is a chance to add real value, to step up where no one else is stepping up.

If you volunteer, the Partner will be relieved and impressed. In fact, everyone in the room will be impressed. If you do this consistently, you will quickly develop a reputation as a lawyer who seeks the most challenging assignments. Because you seek the most challenging assignments, Partners will think of you as more valuable than those Associates who do routine work. Your increased value will be rooted in both the unique substantive experience you will be developing, as well as the value of good will you will be building with Partners. Remember, the psychological stress (described above) that Partners feel when assigning novel and complex projects is converted into tremendous relief once they have an Associate on their team who eagerly seeks novel and complex assignments. You will be the source of such relief for the Partner. This emotional component cannot be overstated. See Chapter 5 *The best business advice I ever received.*

If you seek the most complex assignments, both Partners and other Associates will assume that you must be exceptionally talented. In this way the podium effect works to your advantage. Because a Partner has described the project as novel and unusually complex, and because you have sought out such assignment, the clear implication is that you are unusually able to handle novel and complex assignments.

Another outcome of seeking the most complex assignments is that over time, because you are doing assignments that are generally considered out of the ordinary, you will have the most diverse set of skills as among the lawyers of your vintage. This of course creates a virtuous cycle where Partners continue to bring you the most complex assignments and you continue to outpace your colleagues in developing a diverse array of legal knowledge and skills.

You might think that this notion of seeking the most complex assignments is foolish. It puts you at greater risk of not performing well. It also might require additional effort in an already demanding job. Why not simply do a good job on the ordinary assignments? You can advance through the ranks doing a good job on ordinary assignments, so why make the job riskier and harder by taking the most challenging assignments?

Setting aside the fact that I have debunked the myth of the novel and unusually complex project (i.e., all assignments are novel and complex to Junior Associates), the fact is, you may want to seek the most complex assignments as a matter of job security. From a Partner's perspective, Associates doing ordinary work can be replaced as needed, but an Associate doing novel and complex work and who actually seeks out challenging assignments is rare and valuable.

I was in the San Francisco office of a large firm when the dotcom bubble burst in 2002. Many of our corporate Clients put projects on hold or slowed the pace of those projects that were not on hold. Most of the ordinary work dried up for the law firm. Our corporate Clients either were not proceeding with ordinary projects, because of the market disruption, or they were having their internal lawyers do the work given the overall slowdown of activity internally. But the novel and complex projects tended to be very significant to the wellbeing of our corporate Clients; these projects could not be stopped; these projects became even more critical. Furthermore, the complexity of such assignments meant that the internal lawyers were not sufficiently specialized to handle the work or, in many cases, internal lawyers were victims of the podium effect vis-à-vis prestigious law firm Partners telling them that the project was novel and complex. All of these factors combined to mean that my time during the recession of 2002-2003 remained occupied by Client demands; I continued to develop my skills as a lawyer and I continued to develop positive relationships with Partners at my law firm and with Clients. By the time the recession was over it was clear that my future was on much firmer ground than the future of my peers. This exact pattern repeated itself during the Great Recession of 2009-2012.

One situation when an assignment that others were afraid to do came along, and for which I volunteered, was in 1999. At the request of a Client, I wrote a Limited Liability Company Operating Agreement in a fashion that purposefully mimicked a corporation's structure, from scratch, using nothing but a precedent LLC Operating Agreement and a precedent Corporate Charter. The Client wanted the pass-through tax treatment of an LLC, but believed that their investors would be more receptive to traditional corporation concepts. So, instead of "interests" in the LLC, we created "shares" and instead of "managing members" of the LLC, we implemented a "board of directors," and so on. The challenge was not merely nomenclature, but rather the need to draft into the LLC Agreement all of the corresponding concepts under the Delaware Corporations Code and case law that apply to corporations, so that such corporation concepts would apply to the LLC. It was the first time anyone at my firm, perhaps anyone ever, had done so.

Another benefit of taking on the most complicated assignments is that the work is never boring. Over time you will have a greater variety of work than your colleagues. And more of the work you do will be with Partners and Clients that are energized by the novelty and complexity of the issues. The degree to which the Partners and Clients are either energized or bored by their work will correlate to your own sense of enthusiasm or malaise. In my case, there were many days when the work felt overwhelming, but very rarely was it boring. I believe this is because only a fraction of my practice was focused on what others perceived as ordinary. The majority of my work throughout my career was considered by others to be novel and complex.

As I noted above, I volunteered for novel and complex assignments. One of my bosses called me Mikey, because of an old T.V. commercial in which a kid named Mikey eats a new cereal, because Mikey will try anything. The nickname "Mikey" never stuck (thankfully), but the reputation for taking on novel and complex assignments did. After a few years, I was known throughout my practice area as the guy who liked the novel and complex work.

Over time, even Clients saw me this way. The Chief Investment Officer of the largest pension fund in the United States, which is responsible for managing over $300 billion ($300,000,000,000.00) introduced me in a meeting by saying, "this is Paul McCoy, we give him all of the complicated transactions." Once Clients view you as the go-to guy for complicated transactions, your career is set.

Just as it did for me, if you seek the most complicated assignments, you will accelerate your career, create job security for yourself and enhance your enjoyment of being a lawyer.

10

Understand and respect your limits.

This Chapter discusses a commonly ignored pearl of wisdom. It is advice shared throughout the world. It is advice ignored throughout the world. In a law firm, this advice is essential to surviving and ultimately succeeding. You must understand and respect your limits. It is absolutely critical for Junior Associates to understand that nobody, not even their own body, will prevent them from going well past their limits. Burnout is a common ailment in law firms. Burnout is the direct result of not understanding or not respecting your limits.

In this context, **"limits"** means the rate of activity and level of effort that you can endure without harm to your physical or emotional wellbeing. Note that your "limits" are actually elastic, depending on a number of variables not directly tied to the rate of activity or level of effort at work. I will explain this, below. But first, why is it so hard to follow the advice; why is it so hard to understand and respect your limits?

Many people believe this advice is ignored because of fear—specifically, fear that our limits render us incapable of excelling. The common belief is that people want to excel, so they ignore their limits for fear that their limits will prevent them from excelling. There may be some truth in this analysis, but I believe the problem is more nuanced.

The nuanced analysis takes into account two common beliefs that are simply wrong.

The first fallacy that leads people to fail to understand and respect their limits is that people believe that their body will let them know they are approaching their breaking point, as if perhaps their physiology or subconscious mind will somehow protect them from themselves. The belief that your body will let you know your limits before you have exceeded them is wrong. Because we are not talking about the outer most activity and effort possible before dropping dead, your body is at the mercy of your judgment.

The second fallacy is that people believe that their bosses—in a law firm this typically means Partners or Senior Associates—will know how much work is being asked of them and that such bosses will not ask them to do more than is possible. In other words, there is a belief that *other people* will protect them from themselves. It is erroneous to believe that *other people* will protect you from exceeding your limits. When you stop to think about this, it is only logical. How would another person know your limits? You might think that others will see that you have reached your limits when your work begins to suffer or you begin to miss deadlines, but you would be wrong. Any number of reasons could be behind subpar performance. You do not want to wait until a Partner confronts you on such issues to then explain it is because you have exceeded your limits. Saving your reputation at that point will not be easy. Further undermining the fallacy that other people will help you avoid exceeding your limits is the fact that in a law firm structure many different people may have you working on many different projects. You are unlikely to have the luxury of a single boss giving you all of your assignments. As such, there is no way for any one person to know how much is being asked of you in total. Only you can know how much is being asked of you in total. But even if you land in a situation where a single Partner is giving you all of your work, the fact remains that only you can understand your limits. It is entirely your responsibility to understand and respect your limits.

Understanding your limits requires self-examination, introspection, reflection and close self-monitoring. To do this you must consider a wide range of factors, such as the timeframe, diet, sleep habits, exercise and socializing.

Timeframe? That's probably an aspect you haven't heard or seen mentioned before. Your limits are probably different when considering a 24-hour period than a one-year period. In fact, it is precisely because your limits differ depending on the timeframe that you might fall victim to burnout if not careful. Most lawyers have in their past crammed for an exam, perhaps studying all night and then taking the exam on zero sleep. Many have gone days in a row with only four or five hours of sleep. My opinion is that from time to time this is not harmful and can be strategically helpful for achieving an academic goal or meeting a work deadline. But such behavior can be destructive, particularly if you lose track of the frequency with which you are depriving yourself of sleep. This can put you at serious risk of inadvertently depriving yourself of so much sleep that your body, particularly your brain and nervous system, begin to malfunction. It happened to me.

In 2001, I was working on a merger of two telecommunications companies in Brazil. The combined new company was planning to participate in a government-run auction process bidding for telecommunications rights. Although I was a Junior Associate at the time, the Partner felt I had been doing a good job and had invited me to join him on the business trip to Brazil to represent the Client in person during the auction process. The opportunity to travel internationally for business was then, and remained throughout my career, a huge incentive to perform well. When this opportunity came my way, I decided I would redouble my efforts: I would work harder, pulling even more all-nighters, and I would push myself even harder to complete my projects as close to perfectly as I could. The problem was that I was already at or exceeding my limits at work. Deciding to pull more all-nighters and push myself even harder to get every project done perfectly was a bad idea. One day, seemingly out of nowhere, I was struck with an overwhelming sensation of panic and confusion. My heart was racing and my mind seemed to be thinking dozens of thoughts simultaneously. Irrationally, I was trying to solve every legal issue in every one of my projects simultaneously, and even more irrationally, I had convinced myself that my entire career depended upon me doing so! A friend of mine explained to me that I was having a panic attack and that I needed to take it a little easier at work. "So panic attacks are real!" was my first thought. (How arrogant I was to dismiss the many times other people had shared with me the fact that they had had a panic attack.) My second thought was, "oh, thank God it's just a panic attack. I thought I was going crazy."

Because the excruciating experience of having a panic attack happened to me as a result of exceeding my limits at work, my knee-jerk reaction was to immediately put the brakes on at work, as recommended by my friend. But, just as I had taken working to the extreme, I took my retreat to the extreme. I requested not to go on the business trip to Brazil, removing myself from that project and removing myself from several other projects, in order to right-size my workload. I also phoned-in that I was taking a week's vacation, starting immediately. In hindsight, I clearly overacted. I had no choice, really, because I had never contemplated my limits and so when I exceeded them the only action I could take was to overact in the other direction. Had I known my limits, I would not have exceeded them in the first place. But suppose I did exceed my limits, even knowing them: I would have been in a very good place to know how to dial back my efforts in a manner that would have been far less disruptive to my colleagues at the firm.

I believe that my path to exceeding my limits was due, in part, to depriving myself of the sleep I needed. Whether I learned it in movies or by believing the exaggerations of colleagues, I thought working non-stop and pushing for perfection was what it took to make it in a large law firm. This required finding time from anywhere—fewer social activities, less exercise activities and less sleep. I thought an hour or two a day carved from my sleep and added to my work was just what I needed to excel. What's more, I believed others were doing exactly as I was. In my view, I was merely mimicking the behavior of others, and I was doing so on the assumption that my limits must be similar to their limits. If they didn't need much sleep, neither did I. If they could push for perfect work under stressful timelines and very little sleep, so could I. I was wrong.

Once I began to analyze my limits, I realized I was not taking very good care of myself all around. My health regimen could be summarized as a poor diet, frequent sleep deprivation and very little exercise. Much has been written about the importance of diet, sleep habits and exercise, so I will not attempt to go into details on these topics in this book, other than to say that I learned that if you eat healthy foods, prioritize sleep and exercise regularly you will have significantly increased the likelihood of having the stamina required to survive and succeed in a law firm.

I would like to add socializing to the common list of self-care steps (i.e., diet, sleep and excise). The importance of socializing is rarely discussed in the context of understanding your limits, but socializing is critical to maintaining the stamina required to survive and succeed in a law firm. During my seventh and eight years as an Associate, I skipped several important social events—three weddings of three very good friends. These friends lived far away and these weddings occurred in Indonesia, Poland and Thailand. In each instance, work was moving so fast and my responsibilities felt so significant that I simply could not (or so I believed) leave for a week to go to the various destination weddings. So, I skipped those weddings. I worked vigorously towards promotion to Partner. After I made Partner, I obtained a copy of the internal memorandum written in support of my promotion to Partner. Nowhere, not even in vague terms, was the fact that I skipped three weddings of dear friends mentioned. I was stunned to learn that there are no career bonus points for social self-deprivation.

Not only are there no bonus points for social self-deprivation, the fact is that attending social events, spending time with friends and family, allowing your mind to focus on aspects of life other than work, is critical to maintaining the stamina required to survive and be successful at a law firm. In my case, after I realized that I was gaining nothing, and risking everything, by depriving myself of a social life, I began to prioritize friends and family. My career took off. Coincidence? I don't think so.

Above, I expose two fallacies that result in Junior Associates failing to respect their limits. But there is another problem. The vast majority of people have not closely examined and therefore fail to understand their limits. I believe if people really understood their limits, they would rarely, if ever, exceed those limits. The long-term harm so clearly outweighs any short-term gain; no rational person would take the risk.

Learning your limits is a process of experimentation and observation. It is similar to the scientific method, in fact. Because it is a process of experimentation and observation, the sooner you begin the better off you will be. You do not want to find yourself several years into a career approaching burnout and then start to conduct your experiments and observations.

The experiments you conduct to understand your limits should include all of the factors I noted above: timeframe, diet, sleep habits, exercise and socializing. You must experiment with changes in each and closely observe how you feel. If you are still in law school and reading this book, great! You can most easily mix and match changes in these variables in the many weeks of law school during which there are no exams. Closely observe how you feel as you tinker with the amount of sleep you get, the kind of food you eat, the frequency and type of exercise you enjoy and the nature and frequency of your social activities.

Many reading this book will already be lawyers. I understand the hesitance to conduct such experiments while handling the workload of a law firm Associate. For you, the experiments must be subtle and observation of your moods and energy level will be the best way for you to learn about your limits. For example, you may be forced to work very late into the nights on a project. That will be an excellent time to observe yourself in respect of your limits for sleep deprivation. How do you feel each day? How is your mood and energy level? Then, at another point in time, you may need to work for twenty or thirty days in a row, without any days off. During such a stretch, you might be able to go to bed at a reasonable hour, but you might find that the project requires your involvement every day. This will be an excellent time to observe yourself in respect of diet, exercise and socializing. Are you eating more junk food as the consecutive days of work add up? Are you skipping exercise? Are you skipping or cancelling social activities? How are all these factors impacting your mood and energy?

It takes time, so be patient with yourself. Observation is the key. Consider keeping a work journal that tracks what you are working on, how hard you are working, and how each of the key factors are impacted (i.e., timeframe, diet, sleep habits, exercise and socializing).

Keep in mind that the process of understanding your limits is not binary. It is not as if one day you discover, Eureka!, I understand my limits! But rather, every time you observe yourself and consider the key factors, you evolve one small step in your understanding of your limits. The results are very subtle, but very powerful over time. Your understanding of your limits will become second nature after a while, and once understood, your decision to respect such limits will become as close to instinctive as any aspect of human behavior.

Without engaging in the process of learning your limits, sadly, the degradation of your wellbeing is so gradual that you may not even notice it until it is too late. There are alarming rates of depression and anxiety disorders in the legal profession, as well as substance addictions and other harmful diseases. I am convinced all of these are directly attributable to, or at least exacerbated by, the failure of lawyers to understand and respect their limits.

11

Trust life's process.

In 2007, I was on the phone with a friend. I was bemoaning my existence. I had been working extremely long hours and, what was worse (far worse) is that the Client lording over me was ruthless and unreasonable. I was a Senior Associate at the time and very dedicated to being promoted to Partner. But law firms rarely make promises to Associates about making Partner. At best, one receives a vague statement that they are "on track" or "in good standing" or "doing everything right." But rarely have I heard a law firm promise an Associate that he or she will be made Partner. And on the rare occasions where the promise is made, it is phrased as a promise without a timeframe. I myself, once I had some credibility as a Partner, told very promising Associates that in my view they would make Partner, but that the question was *when* not *if*. In other words, I tried to reassure them that they had the intelligence, skill and dedication to make Partner, but it was not possible to know when they would make Partner.

So, there I was in 2007 working extremely hard with no assurance it would be worth it in the long run. I was a Senior Associate struggling with workload and Client demands and I just couldn't stomach the idea of working so hard for such Clients without having a promise that it would all pay off. I told my friend about incident after incident of my total dedication to getting projects done. And I whined on and on about not having any promise that the work would result in my promotion to

Partner. I explained to my friend that it felt like I had everything to lose, the law firm had everything to gain, and I was at risk of getting seriously screwed.

My friend listened for a while and after I had sufficiently vented, he said something that I will never forget. He said, "you don't trust life's process, do you?"

It was such an odd question. Do I trust life's process? I thought to myself, "is life's process something one does or doesn't trust?" I mean, to me life was just life and its process was just the byproduct of whatever happens. Boy did the puzzle pieces begin to fall into place as I began to think about his question.

Life's process. I mulled over this concept for days, weeks, months. I still mull over it from time to time. It's a huge concept. It is essentially the interplay between fate and free will.

And then to ask if I trust life's process. Mind blown.

Clearly, until that moment I had not trusted life's process. I was so distrusting that I thought I might work harder than my colleagues, volunteer for the most complex assignments, navigate the personalities of the most ruthless and demanding Clients and still not get promoted to Partner. Furthermore, I didn't trust that if that actually happened, if I was denied promotion to Partner, there might be something else rewarding and fulfilling for me to do with my life. The more I thought on this question, the more I realized I didn't trust any aspect of life's process. The more I analyzed it, however, the more I realized I had no basis to distrust life's process. Nearly everything in my life had unfolded in a logical way. Some good, some bad, some objectively fair and some objectively unfair. But always within the bounds of rational comprehension. I realized that, in retrospect, life has a process.

Discovering that life has a process was a game changer for me. I decided it was in my best interest to trust life's process. To trust that all of my hard work and dedication would result in promotion to Partner and that if it didn't, well that would mean I was destined to achieve something else in life. I let go of all of the "what if" questions about the possible ways I might be screwed over by my law firm. Letting go of these concerns freed up a lot of mindshare for me to focus on other things. It freed me to focus on other aspects of my work, and importantly it freed me to focus on other aspects of my life, which is critical to long-term wellbeing. See Chapter 10 *Understand and respect your limits.*

How does all of this fit into surviving and being successful at a law firm? Simple. When doubts creep in about whether or not all of the hard work and sacrifices are worth it, trust life's process. When doubts creep in about whether or not you are doing a good job, trust life's process. When doubts creep in about whether or not you are liked by your colleagues, trust life's process. When doubts creep in about whether or not you are as smart as others, as capable as others, or as strong as others, trust life's process.

12

Law firm careers evolve slowly, like inverted dog years.

It is folk wisdom that each human year is 7 years of a dog's life. Well, we might also say that every year for a Junior Associate at a law firm is like 7 years of a normal human's life. In other words, life at a law firm unfolds slowly, like inverted dog years—it takes seven years in a law firm to feel the same sense of forward momentum as others feel in one year. Time is experienced differently for lawyers at a law firm, because change during the career of a lawyer at a law firm happens at a glacial pace. Consider the fact that in the entire career of a law firm Partner they are likely to have only two titles: Associate and then Partner. Sure, there are subtle distinctions made in conversations inside law firms, such as Junior Associate, Senior Associate, Junior Partner, Senior Partner, but look at the website of any law firm and you will see that the vast majority of lawyers have only one of two official titles: Associate and Partner. There is a growing number of "Of Counsel" and other titles at law firms, primarily for those who have grown beyond being an Associate but who are not promoted to Partner (whether at their choice or the law firm's choice). Even in such cases, those lawyers will have had only two titles in their careers: i.e., Associate and then Of Counsel.

With so little change in title, it is easy to feel as though life is dragging on in stasis, forever. Each day, you awake and tackle the demands of the day. Emails, phone calls, conference calls, meetings, drafting, research, as well as all the layers of social dynamics within the law firm and throughout your universe of friends and family and the world at large. All the mundane things in life, happening again and again and again, day after day after day. The exciting things are few and far apart. In the typical first five years of a lawyer's career, he or she is likely to have only one major life event: Marriage. In other respects, his or her life will seem the same. Same firm. Same title (Associate). Same area of practice. Same people at the office, albeit some will come and some will go, but overall the sameness smothers any changes.

Just as the frequency of receiving graded feedback on assignments, quizzes and tests declined from high school to college, and just as the frequency of receiving graded feedback on assignments, quizzes and tests declined from college to law school, so to the frequency of feedback declines again upon joining a law firm. Formal feedback declines to almost zero, other than the annual performance review and those infrequent moments when you have either done truly extraordinarily good work or royally screwed something up. By the fifth annual performance review you will realize that there is a certain sameness in the performance reviews, too. If you are doing well, you will be told you are doing well. Not much more will be said. If you are not doing well, you will be told the ways in which you are not doing well. This can get quite detailed, but we need not spend time on that scenario, because anyone motivated enough to read this book is very likely to receive good performance reviews at a law firm.

Given so much sameness in the day-to-day life of a lawyer, it is important to teach yourself to recognize the vast amount of change that is in fact occurring. You will be growing a tremendous amount from year to year, regardless of the sameness in title and the sameness of office and so on. From time to time, reflect on the type of work you are doing and how it is becoming more advanced over time. Reflect on the interactions you have with Partners and ultimately with Clients, which will shift slowly and subtly. If you do not reflect on such things, you might not notice that your interactions with Partners and Clients have shifted from receiving and implementing instructions as a First-Year Associate to collaborative problem solving as a Mid-Level Associate. You might not notice how jargon that seemed foreign and intimidating becomes second nature. You might fail to realize that you have fully transitioned from being a law student to being a lawyer. Analyzing the ways in which you have grown will give you greater job satisfaction and dispel any concerns you may have that your career has stalled or is off track.

Another technique to fend off the long periods between constructive feedback is to focus on micro-feedback, such as taking notice—perhaps even in your work journal—of what goes well (or not) for you during depositions, trials, mediations and presentations. Any project can be the source of feedback, if you take the initiative to conduct a self-assessment. And I would say it is not excessive to seek feedback from Partners quarterly, so long as you take the initiative and have prepared questions to discuss with them. For example, you could ask Partners to tell you three strengths they see in you and three weaknesses. Be open to the feedback, which is harder than it sounds. Then work on the weaknesses, of course. Three months later, go back to those Partners and repeat the exercise. You will see how you are growing as a lawyer and, importantly, the Partners will see how you are growing as a lawyer.

13

Cynicism is cancer of the soul and it's contagious.

I would wager that 80% of cynical lawyers never make Partner in law firms. Maybe this is a causal relationship, in that somehow being cynical works against becoming a Partner. Maybe cynicism is a natural reaction to the subtle awareness in some lawyers that they are never going to make Partner. Perhaps it is some combination of the two. Regardless, it is important to steer clear of cynics, as I will explain in this Chapter.

It is important to distinguish cynicism, skepticism and pessimism. **"Cynical"** is defined as distrustful of human sincerity or integrity. **"Skeptical"** is defined as not easily convinced. **"Pessimism"** is defined as a tendency to see the worst aspect of things or believe that the worst will happen. All of these seem negative, but in the practice of law there is healthy skepticism and occasionally a practical application for pessimism. But there is no good place for cynicism. Let's look at each in turn, starting with skepticism, then pessimism and then cynicism.

Can you imagine hiring a lawyer who is not a skeptic, at least when it comes to facts? A lawyer who is not a skeptic would be easily convinced of the facts. The negotiations would go something like this:

Client: The adverse party is using my patent without my consent.

Attorney: I called the adverse party, and they say they are not using your patent without your consent. I believe them. I don't see any case here.

It's absurd, right? Clearly, a good lawyer must be skeptical of facts as presented by an adverse party. And, in fact, a good lawyer must be skeptical of facts as presented from his own Client, too. It should be difficult for either party to convince a good lawyer of the facts, because a good lawyer should dig into the facts for himself until he is satisfied that he has a full understanding of all relevant facts. Healthy skepticism in a lawyer will prevent unpleasant surprises from surfacing during trials or negotiations. Of the three qualities (i.e., skepticism, pessimism and cynicism), it is skepticism that is most useful to a lawyer and beneficial to a career in a law firm.

Now, let's consider a lawyer who is a pessimist. This lawyer would see the worst aspect of things and believe that the worst will happen. This is not a great quality in a lawyer, but for some, pessimism is a powerful motivator. Consider the following conversation:

Client: The adverse party is using my patent without my consent.

Attorney: I am sure they are, but it will be very difficult to prove. I will need to dedicate considerable energy and resources to win this one, because, to be honest, it is a long shot!

The answer from the attorney, above, could be a little off-putting for a Client, but pessimism is in fact motivating the lawyer to work very hard to win. Motivation to win is a quality every Client should want in a lawyer. Pessimists are not much fun to be around, and they are not likely to have leadership roles in law firms, but a pessimist is very capable of surviving and succeeding in a law firm.

Now, let's consider a cynic. This is a person who does not trust human sincerity or integrity. The conversation might go something like this:

Client: The adverse party is using my patent without my consent.

Attorney: You probably do not have a patent and, in any event, I suspect you are trying to use my skills to defraud your competition from engaging in their own business. You will likely have me spend many hours working on your case and then ultimately not pay for my legal services.

The above conversation shows an attorney-Client relationship that is dead before it has even started. A true cynic is unhelpful to Clients, which means unhelpful to a law firm. But the primary reason cynics are bad for a law firm and unlikely to survive or succeed at a law firm is not related specifically to their ability to serve Clients. The primary reason cynics are bad for a law firm and unlikely to survive or succeed at a law firm is that they are damaging to the wellbeing of everyone else working in the law firm.

A cynic cannot trust human sincerity or integrity. My belief is that cynics are themselves lacking in sincerity and integrity and thus believe everyone else is similarly insincere and untrustworthy. For example, if the law firm made an announcement of a new policy that benefited all employees, the cynic would say it was only done for underhanded reasons that benefited the Partners at the expense of everyone else. The cynic would believe this, because it is the only explanation consistent with how the cynic himself would behave. Because the cynic lacks sincerity and integrity, he assumes all others lack sincerity and integrity and is constantly projecting insincerity and untrustworthiness onto everyone else at the law firm.

Cynicism is reinforced by the misguided and warped perceptions of cynics. Cynics have an uncanny ability to reinterpret any event or fact to fit their delusions. While a cynic is young, vitality neutralizes the damaging effects of cynicism. Over time, however, the unrelenting corruption of cynicism overpowers the enthusiasm of youth. A young cynic is sometimes considered insightful, sophisticated or even poetic. An old cynic is always considered paranoid, backward and blathering. Cynicism, the very essence of distrust of human sincerity and integrity, is a cancer eating away at the souls of cynics. But unlike physical cancer, cynicism is contagious.

I have observed colleagues whose offices were nearby to a true cynic's. Slowly but surely those colleagues' views and attitudes towards all other human beings began to turn cynical. Cynics tear people down. As a result of interacting with the cynic, such colleagues began to shift into cynicism themselves.

Because cynicism is contagious, it spreads, and as it spreads the amount of discord and contention within the law firm grows. As discord and contention grow, a number of bad things happen. People do not work well together, making teams less effective. Less effective teams produce less revenue. Meanwhile, the sense of fulfillment and reward justly earned in a legal career is diminished, because nothing good is any longer perceived as good;

rather, there is always a cynical explanation for anything good. Cynicism slowly eats away at the soul of law firm culture just as it does the human soul. As the environment shifts, talented lawyers who are sincere and have integrity, and who believe that most other humans are sincere and have integrity—i.e., those who are not themselves cynics—leave the law firm in search of likeminded lawyers.

It would be very difficult advice to implement if I were to say, "don't be a cynic." A true cynic most likely needs psychotherapy to reorient his or her worldview. As such, my advice is for all of the non-cynics. The advice is simple. Stay as far away from cynics as you can, and do so as soon as you can. Surround yourself with people who are sincere and have integrity and thus view others as having sincerity and integrity.

A quick note for the skeptics, because I know it is not easy to convince you and you may find faults in my analysis above. My analysis is purposefully oversimplified. I suspect everyone exists on a spectrum in respect of each quality discussed in this Chapter. For example, it seems unlikely anyone is completely devoid of any cynicism. Imagine how naïve one would be if one believed *all* humans were *always* sincere and that *all* humans *always* had integrity. In fact, such worldview would not allow for healthy skepticism, which as noted above is an important quality in a good lawyer. Similarly, imagine someone who is *100% optimistic*; someone who *always* assumed the best aspects of things and believed that *only* the best outcomes will happen. Such worldview would likely result in under-preparation for trials and negotiations, and thus such a person would likely be unpleasantly surprised to lose trials and negotiations; such a person would be very likely to have unhappy Clients and, eventually, no Clients.

So, for the skeptics, I will finetune my advice, as follows: Stay as far away as possible from any person who demonstrates an unusual level of cynicism, and do so as soon as you identify them as being such a person. Surround yourself with people who are, for the most part, sincere and have integrity and thus view others as being, for the most part, sincere and trustworthy.

14

You are no longer paying others; you are now being paid.

You may not have realized it, but from the time you entered preschool all the way through graduating from law school, you were paying others to provide a service to you—i.e., to teach you. This dynamic changes once you join a law firm. From the first minute you join a law firm, you are being paid to provide a service. This is a fundamental shift that is ignored entirely by the legal profession year after year as students go from law schools to becoming lawyers at law firms. It is among the most significant paradigm shifts you will encounter in your life.

The reason I make a big deal about this paradigm shift is that, in my experience, 90% of the complaints young Associates have at law firms sound very much like the kind of complaints students might have if a faculty was not meeting the needs of the students. In other words, in my experience, 90% of Associates' complaints are rooted in a failure to appreciate the paradigm shift from paying others, on the one hand, to being paid by others, on the other hand.

During my tenure as a Partner, young Associates approached me from time to time with requests (often thinly disguised complaints) relating to the numerous opportunities for Partners to improve the lives of Associates. These complaints came in two styles: (i) ways in which the law firm should spend money on Associates and (ii) how Partners should be spending their time to make the lives of Associates easier. Of course, the complaints were never characterized this way by the Associates, because the two buckets I have identified above reflect the business realities of a law firm and most Junior Associates do not think about the business realities of a law firm. See Chapter 19 *Understand your law firm's management and economic structures.*

In response to complaints implicating the first category, above, I would ask how much of the Associates' salaries would they be willing to dedicate to the idea? It was very rare for Associates to agree to a reduced salary in order for more money to be spent on them in other ways.

In response to complaints implicating the second category, above, I would ask whether or not the idea was worth redirecting Partners' time from Client development? Few Associates were prepared to answer this question, but many simply said "yes" blind to the consequences of what such redirection would mean for the success of the law firm. At which point, we would have a deeper conversation about law firm economics.

My goal in this Chapter is to help you avoid making suggestions without first carefully considering the implications for the law firm, as a whole. I will itemize some of the requests I heard frequently, so that you can think twice before suggesting these to a Partner at your law firm:

> *Technology*. I assure you that every law firm spends a considerable amount of time analyzing the costs and benefits of upgrading their technology. Any suggestions you might have about improving the technology at your law firm should be thought through carefully. If you have identified a technology that would genuinely improve the law

firm's efficiency or effectiveness, and you have thought through the costs of such technology, including any disruptions to current workflow, then of course it is fine to make a presentation of your idea to one of the Partners at your law firm. But be careful, because half-baked ideas and pie-in-the-sky ideas do little more than highlight your inexperience.

Food. Law firms use many different approaches to providing food for Associates, usually for special lunch meetings and often for dinners if Associates are working late at the office. Some law firms reimburse Associates for such dinners, other law firms have food prepared or provided on the premises. The first law firm I worked for had its own cafeteria where food was available at cost (i.e., no markup) to employees. The second law firm I worked for converted one of the conference rooms into a buffet styled dinner each evening at 7 p.m. And the third and final law firm at which I spent most of my career would reimburse Associates who ate dinner at (or near) the office when working late. What you should understand is that for many years law firms have been considering different approaches to making sure food is available to their Associates, particularly in the evenings given the frequency with which Associates must work well past a traditional dinner hour. If you have suggestions about food, make sure they are original, affordable and easy to implement before approaching Partners with such suggestions.

Bonding Events. I would be shocked if any law firm did not understand the importance of having events from time to time to create cohesion and comradery among the

Associates, and among the Partners together with Associates. The key tradeoff is, as always, the cost of the event. Frequency is a factor, too. A relatively inexpensive gathering once a month in a conference room to share food and drink might be within a law firm's budget. Champagne and caviar at the Ritz each week are likely not within a law firm's budget. My advice is that before you suggest bonding events, do a little digging to see what events already occur. Furthermore, ask yourself if the real purpose of the bonding event is for you to get together with a small subset of your friends at the law firm and have the law firm pay for it. These kinds of tricks are transparent; Partners know what you are doing. Nearly every idea you have in this area has already been thought and most have been tried.

Attending Seminars. This might have been the topic Associates were most adamant about when making suggestions to me. They approached me and explained the enormous benefits to the law firm if the law firm would pay for them to attend XYZ seminar. And sometimes this is true, but again it depends on the costs and benefits in question. You would be shocked at the number of times people approached me to approve ideas that were outrageous. One example, out of many, was a young Associate who asked for approval to go to a seminar in Luxembourg. The request was to cover expenses for the airline tickets, a hotel room, meals and the *coup de gras* was the price of admission to the seminar. The seminar was a "Superior Event" and thus had a superior price tag: $10,000. So, all in all, I was being asked to send a Junior Associate to Luxemburg, all expenses paid, including $10,000 seminar admission. This would have been at least $15,000 all in, and what would the law firm get out of it? A happy Associate? Sure, we like Associates to be happy. An informed Associate? Again, we like those, too. An Associate who may have made some connections? Great. Yet, the harsh truth is that law firms would like to believe that the high salaries paid to Associates, together with other critical areas of law firm culture, keeps Associates happy. And law firms expect Associates to stay informed without the benefit of overpriced seminars. Finally, law firms expect Associates over time to develop connections. So, from the law firm's perspective, everything the Associate seeks is already expected without the $15,000 price tag. In the end, all that resulted from the Associate's request to attend the seminar in Luxembourg, was that my view of the Associate was ever-so-slightly diminished. I was happy he sought out a work-related activity beyond the projects he was handling for Clients, but I was disappointed at the lack of judgment and the sense of entitlement he demonstrated in requesting such an extravagant trip. He could have, instead, requested to attend a local, reasonably-priced seminar, which would have required no travel or lodging expenses, and perhaps offered to give the rest of the team a presentation after the seminar on what he learned. That, I would (and often did) approve.

Car Services. This was a hot topic for many years. A strangely-rewarding perk of working for a top law firm used to be ordering a black town car at the end of the day for a supple ride home. Thankfully, with all the rideshare companies in business today, nobody seems to rely on the car services any longer and the ongoing debate of costs versus benefits has been set aside. I include this paragraph in this book solely to say that in the age of Uber, Lift, etc., it would seem foolish to seek reimbursement for an expensive town car or limousine.

Partner Presentations. This topic is tricky, because good Partners should be interacting daily with Associates and providing specific feedback, guidance, training, mentoring and more. How and when that occurs will vary greatly from Partner to Partner, because they have unique time limitations, work demands, homelife demands, personal wellbeing demands, all just as Associates do. In addition to ongoing interaction between Partners and Associates, most law firms have Partners present to Associates on a wide range of topics as part of training and periodic firm updates. So, broadly speaking, Associates have plenty of Partner attention.

Notwithstanding such attention, Associates would still make requests for practice area leaders, team leaders and office managing partners to hold more meetings or videoconferences. Usually, this request was made out of a desire by the Associates to stay as informed as such law firm leaders in respect of developments at the law firm, the law firm's Clients, and even more broadly with respect to current events. I confess, when I was an Associate, I really wanted the head of our practice area to hold such meetings or videoconferences. It was so painfully obvious how much such person could teach us all. But I realized, thankfully before I made the suggestion, that it was an arrogant idea. The notion that I, as an Associate, needed to be as informed as the law firm's practice area leader on such matters is absurd. And there are better ways to keep

> up with developments at the law firm, the law firm's Clients and current events without asking a Partner, particularly a Partner in a leadership position, to dedicated precious time (in a profession where time is literally money). So, my advice is to attend all firm-related meetings, training and conference calls when scheduled, but think twice before suggesting that Partners make additional presentations at additional meetings or conference calls.

I could go on with other examples that came up from time to time during my tenure as a Partner, such as requests for golf outings (with other lawyers at the law firm, not even with Clients!), tickets to sporting events and so on, but I suspect you get the idea by now.

There is one final story I want to share, however, because it is my favorite. A first-year Associate approached a Senior Partner and explained with all sincerity that her performance in high school, college and law school had been extraordinary in large part because each of these institutions had a fitness center. She asked if the law firm had considered turning one of the building's floors into a fitness center. This person had not been at the law firm even six months when she made this suggestion. The Senior Partner said alarm bells immediately went off in his head. "Really?!" He thought to himself. "Take an entire floor of Class A city real estate, currently occupied by fee-generating law firm professionals, and turn it into a fitness center?!" The Senior Partner smiled and said, "Yes, of course we have considered it, but it is not possible." He said this with a very calm demeanor and no explanation; there was no point expending any energy on this question, because there was no point expending any energy on such a clueless Associate. The outcome of the preposterous suggestion was that the Senior Partner suspected that the law firm had, perhaps, hired a problem when they hired this particular Associate. Any Associate who would make this kind of suggestion was likely to be out of touch in other ways, too.

Over time I came to realize that the worldview from which outlandish suggestions were made by Associates was a worldview shaped by an entire life of being in institutions in which others were paid to be there, either directly, as tuition, or indirectly as taxes. In every stage of life in such institutions, a young person is being served; and the people serving are being paid to do it. Everything changes when you begin to understand that it is you who are being paid by the law firm to provide services.

When you realize that the paradigm has shifted such that you are no longer paying others to provide a service to you, but rather you are now being paid by a law firm to provide services to others, you will then be ready to understand that the entire reason for your being hired by a law firm is to improve the profitability of the law firm. While most law firms try to bring new Associates onboard and up to speed in a kind and gentle manner, never forget the bottom line for any law firm is the profits of such law firm; the bottom line will always be the bottom line.

Before you ask any questions or make any suggestions, keep in mind that the best question you can ever ask is, "How can I help?" and the best suggestion you can ever make is a suggestion that has you front and center doing something to make the law firm more profitable.

Note that the advice in this Chapter applies to your parents, too. It is rare, but there are parents who seem to forget the dynamics of a law firm, on the one hand, and their child as an employee of the law firm, on the other hand. So-call
ter Parents" have been known to call law firms and
behalf of their children. Of course, law firms cann
status of such employees at the law firm. To the

employees are not children, they are adults who are employees of the law firm. The law firm could no more discuss issues related to an employee with the parents of such employee than they could discuss issues related to an employee with total strangers. It's completely inappropriate. It reflects poorly on the young Associates such parents are trying to help. So, if you think you might have the kind of parents who would reach out directly to a law firm on your behalf, please warn them not to do so.

15

Nobody is monitoring you daily or weekly.

Generally, you will receive feedback as an Associate in a law firm in three instances: (i) when you make a mistake, (ii) when you do an extraordinarily good job on a project, and (iii) once per year at your performance review. Otherwise, there is a lot of silence when it comes to your performance. Everybody is focused on handling cases and transactions. No matter how much experience a lawyer has, zealously representing Clients occupies one's time and mind thoroughly. Partners and Senior Associates, like everyone else, are very busy. Nobody is monitoring your daily, or even weekly, activities.

I point this out, because from the very first day at a law firm you must begin evolving into an entirely self-sufficient, problem-solving machine. You must develop discipline regarding the use of your time, both at work and in your personal life. In other words, you must take complete ownership for your success or failure in the law firm.

From your very first day with a law firm, you are likely to be given your own office. It will be small, but it will be yours. You could, if you wanted, go into your office and close your door every day. If you do so, it is likely that you will not be very busy. Only work foisted upon you by a Partner or Senior Associate who is desperate for help will make its way to you. This is because if you hide in your office with the door closed, you will not be top of mind for the Partners and Senior Associates. If you are not top of mind, nobody thinks of you for new assignments. Exacerbating the situation is that a closed door generally signals to others that you are very busy, which makes it even less likely that you will be assigned new work. So, there you sit, in your own office with your door closed doing far less work than you would otherwise. If this seems at all appealing, beware. You are setting a trap for yourself that is almost impossible to escape.

Let me explain. As you sit in your office day after day, week after week, feeling blessed to receive such a high salary for doing so little work, eventually you will wonder, "Don't the Partners know how lazy I am being? Don't they know how low my billable hours are? Don't they know I am not busy after so many weeks?"

Here's a fact not known by many Associates: Only a few Partners will keep track of Associates' billable hours in your practice area at your law firm. Most Partners have only a vague idea if you have high or low billable hours. But if your billable hours drop low enough for long enough, it will catch up to you. The process is as follows: You bill your time for the work you do. That time is tracked by software. About a week after the end of each month, a report is circulated to the Partners who hold relevant leadership positions. If you are a new Associate and your hours are low, it is not likely to create concern. This is because most law firms permit a ramp-up period. The leadership Partners will watch your monthly billable hours reported and they will be looking to see if you are trending upwards. If so, they generally leave you alone. If your billable hours are below target and are not trending upwards month-to-month, the leadership Partners will become concerned about your billable hours. Once the leadership Partners are concerned, they will reach out to the Partners for whom you have been doing most of your work and ask about you. They will ask if everything is going okay with your integration into the law firm. They will also ask the Partners with whom you do most of your work whether they have had some kind of slowdown in the work they are generating. Obviously, law firm leadership does not want to hold an Associate accountable for low billable hours if the Partners are not generating enough work. But let's assume the Partners have plenty of work and that the only issue is that you have been holed up in your office like a hibernating bear.

After the conversation between the leadership Partners, on the one hand, and the Partners for whom you do most of your work, on the other hand, it will fall to the Partners for whom you do most of your work to reach out to you and ask why your billable hours are so low. Most Partners are decent human beings and so the first set of questions will be about your wellbeing. Is everything okay outside of work? Is there some way the law firm can help you? Then the questions will turn more specific to the law firm and your workload. Do you understand the law firm's expectations for annual billable hours? Do you understand how hard it is to catch up if you fall too far behind? Do you know how to reach out and ask for work? And so on. Once it becomes clear that there is no good reason for your low productivity, you will have established an unenviable reputation as a slacker. In many cases, the slacker reputation can end a career at a law firm.

The slacker reputation is very difficult to shake, even if you start to be more productive. It is not only because first impressions are hard to change, but there is also a destructive downward spiral. Your low billable hours lead people to assume you are a slacker. As new projects come into the law firm, they will not be assigned to a slacker, unless everyone else who has a reputation for being motivated is completely buried with work. As such, your hours will remain low, perhaps even go lower. This will confirm the suspicions of the Partners that you are a slacker, because, after all, they had a talk with you about your hours and yet you are still not trying. You have entrapped yourself in the slacker spiral. The vast majority of Junior Associates who fall into the slacker spiral leave their law firm (either of their own volition or upon being asked to leave) before too long.

There is more to your responsibilities than avoiding the slacker spiral, of course. As noted at the beginning of this Chapter, you must become a self-sufficient, problem-solving machine. The autonomy you are given from the first day of your career also includes deciding how and when to accomplish the tasks that are given to you. Sure, most tasks will have deadlines, but the time between the moment the task is assigned and its deadline is entirely yours to control. And it will not be long before you are given multiple assignments, requiring you to develop skills at prioritizing. Over time, multiple assignments will come from multiple different people and such prioritization will become very challenging. It is one thing for a single boss to give you assignment after assignment after assignment. Eventually you can ask her which to prioritize. But when different people are loading up your plate, it is often the case that they do not know about the other work being given to you. This can easily lead to overload. Learning skills to prevent such overload is a critical reality when nobody is monitoring you daily or even weekly. See Chapter 10 *Understand and respect your limits* and Chapter 16 *The art of saying "no."* for insights on avoiding overload and burnout.

It is in the void of day-to-day existence at a law firm, with nobody monitoring you, where your career is made or broken. You must use all time wisely and take complete ownership for your success or failure in the law firm.

16

The art of saying "no."

Work can pile up quickly at a law firm. There are many people who can assign you work, not just a single boss. There is likely to be any number of Senior Associates and Partners who at any given time can ask you to take on more work. It is important to recognize that such requests are phrased as requests primarily to be polite. The requests are not really requests, they are demands that cannot be declined unless you have a very good reason. Generally, repeatedly declining work will quickly give you a reputation as a slacker—See Chapter 15 *Nobody is monitoring you daily or weekly* for a discussion of the slacker spiral.

But burnout is a real risk in a law firm. See Chapter 10 *Understand and respect your limits.* Logically, this means that you cannot say "yes" to every assignment. How do you reconcile the fact that saying "no" gives you a reputation as a slacker, but saying "yes" will lead to burnout?

You must learn to say "no" without actually saying "no." This is about as close to metaphysical as you get in a law career. When you are overwhelmed with work and a Partner comes to you with more work, that is when the advice in Chapter 5 *The best business advice I ever received* is critical. Your interaction with the Partner will leave him feeling either good or bad, and he will remember how you made him feel either positively or negatively. He will feel good if you react with gratitude and enthusiasm. He will feel bad if you react with anger or defensiveness. I recommend the following three steps:

1. Let the Partner fully explain the new assignment. Ask questions about it. Show genuine interest in the assignment. After all, you want him to feel that you like working with him and like the kind of work he has to share with you.
2. Tell the Partner about all of the work you currently have on your plate, who assigned it to you and when the various assignments are do.
3. Tell the Partner a date by which you could get his assignment done. If it is not a discrete assignment, but rather a broad request to join a project overall, such as a litigation team, then this step 3 does not apply. Await the Partner's response after you follow No. 1 and No. 2, above.

I can hear you saying, "but you said this was the art of saying 'no.' It sure seems like the steps above leave the outcome open to a 'yes' as much as a 'no.'"

The steps are designed to convey a "yes" attitude, but it is up to the Partner decide if the facts and circumstances require a "no" instead. If he needs his work done faster than you can do it, he will conclude that he cannot assign it to you. If he believes you have too much on your plate already to join his litigation team, he will conclude not to have you join the team. In any case, he will regret not being able to involve you, given how much interest you showed in the project. He might even say "sorry, but I must give the assignment to someone else." If, however, the timing you propose works or your current workload doesn't prevent the level of involvement he needs from you, well then you will receive the assignment and that is all the better because you know the expectations have been set in light of the rest of your workload. Whether you receive the assignment or not, the Partner will leave feeling you are grateful, enthusiastic, hardworking, dedicated and interested in his work, and you will have successfully avoided burnout.

A similar technique, but not really available until you have substantial credibility based on experience, is to explain why a request is not possible and, importantly, to provide a clear explanation of what is possible and how what is possible meets their needs. This is a technique that I used much more often with Clients than colleagues at my law firm. For example, assume a Client asked me for a memorandum summarizing the alternative courses of action they could take and I knew based on experience that such a memorandum would take a week. If the Client asked that it be delivered in a single day, I would first remind myself that the most important outcome in the discussion is how the Client feels. So, I would avoid sounding defensive or bothered by the request, and I would not scoff at the absurdity of the proposed timing. I would, in fact, confirm that I would love to be able to provide such a memorandum in a day. I would then explain a little bit about what needs to happen to prepare the memorandum so that the Client would begin to see it was not possible to do in a day. And then I would suggest a deadline of 10 days out. Because I know that some Clients like to have the last word, my timeline gives the Client the ability to put a little pressure on me and for me to agree to a deadline of one week. What's even better is that my timeline leaves open the possibility that the Client will simply agree to a 10-day deadline. This happens a lot, in fact, because deadlines are often arbitrary and what Clients really want is your service as soon as possible, and the only way for Clients to feel confident that you are providing them priority service is for them to push hard and see what you say is possible under their pressure. Such is the real world.

17

Takers.

I want to warn you about a type of person I call a Taker.

A Taker is a person who takes from you and takes from you and takes from you until you either free yourself from the Taker or die. They are "zoophagus maniacs."[1] Takers do not reciprocate; they do not participate in healthy give and take like normal people; they only take. If they give anything back to you, it is just enough to be able to take more and more from you. They are a kind of human parasite that feeds on the vulnerable good nature of others.

Most human beings want to help others. It is an instinct for most of us. A wise man once said, "the sun does not shine upon itself; the rivers do not drink their own water; everything in nature is meant to provide for others."[2] Takers thrive on manipulating the basic instinct to help others found in most decent people. Takers are in all walks of life, but most relevant to this book is that Takers are at all levels in law firms.

Avoid Takers!

The best thing to do with Takers is ignore them. They are so skilled at manipulating people that if you try to reason with a Taker, they will only make it seem like you are trying to be unhelpful. You cannot reason with or out-reason a Taker. The skills discussed in Chapter 16 *The art of saying "no."* will not work

1. *Dracula*, Braham Stoker (1897).
2. Dalai Lama.

with Takers. The interest you show for a Taker's work will mean nothing to a Taker; the explanation of your current workload will mean nothing to a Taker; and most certainly your effort to explain the date by which you could get a Taker's assignment done will mean nothing to a Taker. Nonetheless, you must attempt to utilize the skills of Chapter 16 before implementing advice of Chapter 18 *The art of "yes-f***ing"* and the advice in this Chapter 17. Your utmost efforts to implement the advice of Chapter 16, and being rejected in doing so, is the only way to be sure that you are dealing with a Taker.

If a Taker is of an equal or lower status than you in the law firm, you can say "no" to whatever unreasonable request is made by the Taker. This is unlikely to transpire, because Takers invariably focus on people beneath them in a hierarchy. Because the Taker you are likely to hear from is a Taker senior to you in the hierarchy, you will feel considerable pressure to capitulate to the Taker's demands.

At some point you will attempt to refuse to continue to give and give and give, while they take and take and take. This is when you will experience the full vile of Takers, because they feed on the energy you use in your attempt to defend yourself. Your discontent is more important to a Taker than the tasks they seek you to do. In the moment you stand up to the Taker, they deploy a dark magic that enables them to reframe the entire situation in a manner that makes the Taker look reasonable and makes you look obstructive and recalcitrant. Thus, the best thing to do with a Taker is ignore them, entirely. Neither say "yes" nor say "no;" simply go radio silent. Sometimes this requires the skills in Chapter 18 *The art of "yes-f***ing,"* but only if the taker is making demands of you in person. If the Taker reaches out to you by email or phone, you can delete such emails and voicemails without replying. You will be amazed how good you feel when you delete an email or voicemail from a Taker.

I had learned about Takers early in my career while at the U.S. Department of the Treasury in Washington, D.C., before going to law school. This was a huge benefit to me early in my legal career. In fact, knowing to disengage from Takers was critical from the very first day I joined one of my law firms.

On my very first day at this particular law firm, after spending the first half of the day at orientation, I went to my office and there was waiting for me a note from a Partner. The note asked that I go to his office when I returned from orientation. And so, I did. The Partner asked me to sit down, but he remained standing. He was pacing a little and began asking me questions. First, he asked if I had taken securities law as a class in law school. I said I had. Then he began asking questions about securities laws, all them very advanced and far beyond what was covered in law school. To each question I didn't know, I simply said, "I don't know." My sense from the beginning of this *tete a tete* was that this particular Partner was on some kind of a power trip. I decided immediately to categorize him as a Taker and act accordingly. Even while calculating silently in my mind how to disengage from this Taker, I kept answering aloud, "I don't know" to each of his ridiculously advanced questions.

Eventually, the Partner got to his point, the moment he was building all along: "Well," he said, "you don't seem to know anything, do you?" His eyes twinkled in satisfaction. He assumed I would be crushed by this comment from such an important Partner as he thought himself to be. The whole situation felt very rehearsed, which made clear to me that it was a routine he played out with others in the past and would likely deploy on others in the future.

I answered, "No, not really."

My tone was devoid of any concern whatsoever. I simply didn't care if this Partner thought I didn't know anything. I wanted to be as useless to this Partner as possible without engaging in direct confrontation and without attempting to explain or reason with him. He was a Taker, and I knew how to handle Takers. Disengage as soon as possible. He paused a few moments. The twinkle was gone from his eye. His tone shifted to that of matter-of-fact business and he gave me a research assignment. I left his office knowing I had made some progress in distancing myself from this Taker, but disappointed that he had given me an assignment. My disengagement was not complete, yet.

The next day, upon arriving back at my desk after the second morning of orientation, I heard the Partner shout from his office, "Paul, come here." His office was only two doors down from mine. I knew he was keen to get from me the results of the research assignment he had given me, and I knew that he was looking for another opportunity to manipulate and torment me. I hadn't done the assignment, because I was *yes-f***ing* him (See Chapter 18). I knew that the sooner I disengaged, the better off I would be.

When I heard him shouting for me, I knew it was a critical moment in my career. If I went to his office on the basis of a shouted summons, I would be under this man's thumb forever. He would ask about the assignment, I would say I hadn't started it, he would ask why, and the downward spiral of engagement would begin. So, I pretended not to hear him. I simply ignored him. He shouted again, louder. I ignored him, again. It must have been obvious I could hear him. The secretaries were looking up from their desks, their eyes shifting from his office to mine as if watching a tennis match. I stared at my computer pretending to work (although my heart rate was up a bit). Finally, he gave up. The Partner simply stopped calling out my name. I was amazed that he didn't even bother to call me on the phone, send an email or walk to my office and ask if I was ignoring him. I suppose he decided I was not going to be his prey and moved on to other, weaker prey.

For years, I congratulated myself for having made that silent stand. Everyone who marched to his orders was miserable, while I worked for other Partners. He brought many people to tears. He threw a stapler at a secretary. He shouted at first year lawyers routinely. He relished in belittling people, often by shaming them publicly in some fashion. He was one of the primary reasons I left that law firm. Even though I never had to work for him, it was unpleasant even being on the same floor with him. There were some good people at that law firm, but the culture overall permitted this Partner to operate the way he did, and I knew in my heart of hearts that it must be better elsewhere. And I was right. It was better, significantly better, at other law firms.

Takers are like humans with talons, and the more you attempt to push back against them, the deeper the talons sink into you. The only defense I know against Takers is total abstention. Ignore them completely. They are a form of bully and if you ignore them, they will move on to find others who will engage in the bully-bullied dynamic. And do not worry that your reputation will be harmed by ignoring Takers. Everyone in a law firm knows who the Takers are. If they complain to others, it will fall on deaf ears.

In my case, I learned over time that my having ignored the Taker in the story I shared with you, above, actually increased the respect others had for me at that law firm. It had enhanced my reputation to have snubbed the Taker.

18

The art of "yes-f***ing."

It is almost a certainty that during your career there will be times when the flow of work exceeds the time you have to get it done. During the early years of your career this might create significant stress, because you do not have the authority to either decline to do such work or to redirect the work to somebody else. In Chapter 16 *The art of saying "no."* I explained a method of neutralizing overwhelming workload requests. I believe the techniques described in Chapter 16 work well with all reasonable people. But, alas, not all Partners are reasonable, so I feel it is my duty to also teach you a technique to use whenever the methods discussed in Chapter 16 fail. There are, unfortunately, some people in this world who are Takers (See Chapter 17 *Takers* for a complete discussion of Takers), and Takers will not be moved by the techniques in Chapter 16. For Takers we need a slightly different approach.

If a Partner comes to you with a project and demands an impossible deadline, particularly at a time when you are already handling a very heavy workload, you must first utilize the techniques discussed in Chapter 16. If those techniques fail, it is safe for you to conclude that you are dealing with a Taker. Chapter 17 explains how to deal with Takers, generally, but here I want to share with you a specific technique to deal with Takers in the heat of the moment, in the very instant that they are crushing you with unreasonable demands, as your blood boils with anger and frustration, which it will because you have made great efforts to be reasonable, positive, enthusiastic, helpful and have sought in return only that they be reasonable. A Taker is never reasonable. And so I emphasize, again, that if and only if the techniques described in Chapter 16 fail, and you are being bullied by a Taker to accept a project while already buried by other work; if you are being pushed by a Taker to accept a project deadline that would be challenging in the best of times and is simply impossible under your heavy workload, and the Taker is purposefully oblivious to your proposals for a win-win as described in Chapter 16; that is the time to implement this Chapter's simple and effective advice: Say "yes."

What?! Can I possibly be recommending that you allow yourself to be destroyed by the impossible work demands of a Taker? No, of course not. In the instance of a Taker, and only in the instance of a Taker, when they are demanding far too much and not open to your reasonable and positive suggestions along the lines of Chapter 16, then you say "yes" to the Taker, but do nothing. You say you will do the assignment and agree to the impossible deadlines and all other outrageous aspects of the Taker's demands, but then you do nothing. You do not do the assignment or any part of it. You put it out of your mind the moment the Taker leaves your office or hangs up the phone and you turn to other matters. The Taker's assignment has been obliviated from your mind, even though you said "yes."

The outcome of this technique is no different for a Taker's Client than had you promised the Taker to do the work and then valiantly tried to do the work, because the Taker's request was already beyond possible. If the assignment is doable, then do it—stressful deadlines do not define a Partner as a Taker. A Taker is defined by demanding the impossible. It should be obvious to you that you cannot use the *yes-f***ing* technique in any circumstance where it might harm a Client. The big difference is not the outcome vis-à-vis a Taker's Client, but rather the improved outcomes for all of the other Clients you are representing at the time. It is their work that will not be undermined or delayed. You will continue to zealously represent them, focusing on their needs. It is also your wellbeing and future that are preserved by using *the yes-f***ing* technique.

You may worry that *yes-f***ing* a Partner will ruin your reputation at your law firm. When you find yourself face to face with a Taker, you can rest assured that you are not the only person the Taker is trying to abuse and exploit. Takers always deserve a good *yes-f***ing*, and all non-Takers in your firm will agree. This is why, once you are sure you are dealing with a Taker, there is no danger to you in *yes-f***ing* the Taker.

I say there is no danger in saying "yes" to a Taker and then doing nothing, because I have experience in seeing how this plays out. The Taker moves on from you, believing that you are working on whatever project they insisted upon—in spite of your efforts to explain your workload and your efforts to create a solution that would work reasonably for you and the Taker—and the Taker will not be back to bother you again until the deadline. When the deadline comes, you simply say the project is not done. The Taker will express considerable disappointment, but it doesn't matter because the Taker can do no harm to your reputation. This is because the Taker already has a terrible reputation of his own—everyone knows he is a Taker; everyone knows he is a bully; the fact that you didn't meet a deadline for the Taker will be either ignored by others or even silently applauded. If the Taker complains about you to the head of your practice area, I assure you that the head of your practice area knows the Taker's reputation and such complaints by a Taker fall on deaf ears. When I was the head of my practice area, Takers would come to me from time to time to complain about an Associate in my Practice Area—and Takers complained more than all other Partners in my law firm combined—and I would listen and not care at all. In fact, in essence I *yes f**ked* them again by making it seem like I cared about their complaints when I knew I wouldn't do a thing about it.

One great thing about the power of *yes-f***ing* is that Takers are incapable of believing they were *yes f**ked*. Their egos are too large. The world revolves around them and so your failure to finish the project on time means only that you are deficient in some way in the Taker's eyes. This is great news. It may seem counter-intuitive at first to think it is good news for a Partner to think you are deficient, but keep in mind that we are talking about a Taker. A Taker who has concluded that you are deficient is very unlikely to ever ask you to take on a project again. Hooray!

Caveats: You must be absolutely sure that you are dealing with a Taker before using the *yes-f**k* technique. Be absolutely sure you tried every technique discussed in Chapter 16 *The art of saying "no."* before concluding any Partner is a Taker. Be absolutely sure that the request is impossible (or extremely unreasonable in light of your existing workload), such that genuinely attempting to complete the Taker's assignment will undermine materially your ability to appropriately complete tasks for other Clients—i.e., the harm of doing the Taker's work is greater to the firm's Clients than the harm of *yes-f***ing* the Taker. If these caveats are all true, then in fact what will have transpired is a Partner will have asked you to complete a task at the risk of harming other Clients, to which you will have attempted to say "no" due to your overwhelming existing workload and the Partner will have simply refused to take "no" for answer—if any harm comes to the Taker's Client as a result, it is clearly the Takers fault, not yours.

*The damage to your reputation if you yes f**k a reasonable Partner is irreparable.*

If you utilize the *yes f**k* technique on non-Takers, the loss of future work you could have received is permanent, and the damage to your reputation is permanent. If you find that you are *yes-f***ing* more than one or two people in a year, which means you have been unfortunate enough to cross paths with more than one or two Takers in a year, either (i) you are wrong in your assessment of who is a Taker or (ii) you are at a law firm with a culture of Takers.

If you have erroneously concluded a person is a Taker, immediately delete the *yes f**k* technique from your toolbox, do not use it again for years and redouble your efforts to get high-quality work done for everyone willing to give you work until you feel you have overcome any damage to your reputation.

If your assessment of Takers has been accurate and you realize that you are at a law firm with a culture of Takers, leave that law firm. Many inexperienced lawyers believe that all law firms are the same, or that all Partners at law firms are the same, and so they believe that the culture at all law firms is the same. Nothing could be farther from the truth. Morgan Lewis was my third law firm, but I stayed there for more than 75% of my career because it had a wonderful culture. I am hopeful that it still does.

19

Understand your law firm's management and economic structures.

Some may be surprised to see me advise Junior Associates to learn their firm's management and economic structures. It is believed by many that the management and economic structures of a law firm are concepts too advanced for new lawyers and not relevant to their survival or success—after all, new lawyers have no input on such matters. New lawyers are paid a salary and if they perform well, they receive bonuses. Some believe that is all new lawyers need to know. The management and economic structures of a law firm, as a whole, are irrelevant, right? Wrong.

The management and economic structures of a law firm dictate how career advancement really works within such law firm.

There are other benefits to understanding your law firm's management and economic structures, but they are not as critical as ensuring your own career success. For example, understanding the management structure may help you understand why certain decisions are made and understand why things are done the way they are done in your law firm. It could also give you clarity on the unspoken hierarchy among Partners. There are many Partners who keep a low profile, at least from the perspective of Associates, but who are incredibly powerful at a law firm. And there are many Partners who enjoy being front and center as often as possible, which tends to give Associates the impression that such Partners are important, but who may have relatively little real power in the law firm. But, in the end, the importance of understanding the management and economic structures of your firm is the impact it has on your career.

I joined Morgan Lewis in 2005 as a sixth year Associate. I became friends with another Associate who was my same class year. His name was Ian. Ian's practice focused on corporate licensing agreements, which is essentially the contracts between corporations that allow one corporation to use assets (usually intellectual property) of another corporation. Although Morgan Lewis has corporate licensing attorneys in many of its offices around the world, the Morgan Lewis team Ian worked with was located in San Francisco. My practice was focused on private investment funds, such as private equity funds, venture capital funds, real estate funds, etc. The team I worked with was dispersed throughout the law firm. Ian and I were both liked by the Partners in our respective practice groups. We both worked very hard; we both had high billable hours; and we both had happy Clients. But the law firm's management and economic structures caused our careers to diverge dramatically.

There are two macro approaches to law firm management and economic structures: Office-by-Office and Practice-Group-by-Practice-Group.

Some law firms are managed on an Office-by-Office basis. In such law firms, the attorneys and staff are managed by a local office managing partner and financial performance is measured by the success (or failure) of the lawyers in each office. Each office in such structure is a separate profit center, which in essence makes each office a miniature law firm within a big law firm. Thus, if an office has lawyers practicing in litigation, corporate securities, intellectual property and myriad other practice areas, the financial success of that office is determined by the aggregate financial success of the lawyers in such office, regardless of such differences in practice area. The various offices are, in turn, under the control of centralized leadership, typically in a home office, and the financial performances of all offices are rolled up to provide the law firm's aggregate performance. In such structure, it is the office managing partners who have significant authority over the career fate of the lawyers in their respective office locations.

The other macro approach to law firm management and economic structures is to use each separate practice group, rather than each separate office, as the basis for law firm management and economics. In 2008, when I was promoted to Partner, Morgan Lewis had many offices (it has even more now), but the offices were <u>not</u> separate profit centers. The law firm was <u>not</u> organized on an office-by-office structure; the separate offices were <u>not</u> miniature law firms. This is critical to understand. Morgan Lewis was organized by practice group. Each practice group was managed as a single business unit across all offices and judged by the performance of that practice group, globally. As such, the litigation practice group was managed on a global basis by a solitary litigation practice group leader and the performance of the litigation practice group was quantified and analyzed on a global basis, aggregating the performance of all litigation Partners located around the world. The same was true for the corporate securities group, the investment management group, the intellectual property group and so on. The various practice groups were, in turn, rolled up to provide the law firm's aggregate performance. In such structure, it is the practice group leaders and not the office managing partners who have significant authority over the career fate of the lawyers in their respective practice groups.

Over time my friend Ian had developed extraordinary relationships with the Partners in the San Francisco office; much better than I had done. But, while I had not developed as strong of relationships in San Francisco, where I was located, I had developed an important relationship with the practice group leader of my practice group who was in our New York office. Ian and I were both eligible for Partnership promotion in 2008. Although Ian had total support from the Partners in the San Francisco office, including the office managing partner in San Francisco, the decision to promote or not promote Ian rested with his practice group leader, who was not located in San Francisco and who did not know Ian well. And although I had less support from the Partners in the San Francisco office (as compared to Ian), the decision to promote or not promote me rested with the leader of my practice group in New York.

You have probably guessed the outcome of this story. Ian was not promoted to Partner. I was promoted to Partner. I am convinced this result was due in part to the fact that I had global practice group leader support in a law firm whose management and economic structure is Practice-Group-by-Practice-Group, whereas Ian had only office leadership support from San Francisco. In a law firm structured on a Practice-Group-by-Practice-Group basis and not an Office-by-Office basis, the outcome was inevitable. Of course, if our firm's management and economic structure had been Office-by-Office, Ian would have been promoted and I might not have been.

If this seems obvious to you and easily handled, you are naïve. The reality is that most Junior Associates receive their work assignments from the Partners in their own office. Typically, the only Partners who know an Associate's quality are the Partners in the Associate's own office. Unless an Associate proactively seeks opportunities to interact with a practice group leader, the Associate will have little, if any, exposure to practice group leaders located in far-off offices.

Year after year I watched as Associates grew false confidence in their career prospects, because the Partners in their local offices thought very highly of them, and year after year I saw Associates get passed up for promotion to Partner, because the practice group leaders had little or no knowledge of them.

The important thing is to know who has the power to support your promotion, not just the desire. It is important that those people who know who you are and think highly of you are also the people who can genuinely champion you for promotion to Partner.

But how to get such people to know you and think highly of you? The easiest way is to make their lives' easier. Reach out to them and offer to do work on their Client matters. There is no easier way to demonstrate your abilities and your dedication to the law firm than to do work specifically for them and their Clients. There is no easier way to win over someone's appreciation than to help them meet the needs of their Clients. Remember, Partners at all levels are swamped with work and have constant anxiety about how to get their projects assigned to high-quality Associates. If you ease their burden, they will be left with the feeling that you are a fantastic lawyer (and they will remember how you made them feel). When decisions begin to be made about who is promoted to Partner and who is not, you can rest assured you will be on the "yes" list.

There are two additional points needed at this juncture in our discussion. First, impressing the right people will help your chances of being promoted, but it does not mean that you can ignore the rest of the Partners. Any respected Partner at any law firm can torpedo any Associate's promotion (fortunately, Takers are never respected in such matters). Each law firm has their own way of ensuring that no Associate is promoted to Partner against the strong wishes of existing Partners. Many law firms use a process whereby an independent reviewing Partner is tasked with preparing a memorandum to set forth all positive and negative input about a Partner candidate after canvassing all current Partners. It is easy to see that a law firm would shy away from promoting an Associate to Partner if one of the current well-regarded Partners had damning things to say about the candidate.

Second, if your law firm is structured on an Office-by-Office basis, then it is the Partners in your office you must impress most of all. If each office is managed independently of each other office, it is very likely that each office is given the autonomy to determine which Associates to promote to Partner in their respective office. If you are in a law firm with an office-by-office management and economic structure, then the Partners in your office are more powerful with respect to your career than Partners elsewhere in your firm.

The analysis is going to vary from law firm to law firm and the important overarching point is for you to find out what management and economic structures apply in your specific law firm. Do not blindly trust that because you are impressing the Partners in your office, you will get promoted. Do not blindly trust that because you are impressing the Partners that have leadership roles in your practice group, you will get promoted. Learn your law firm's management and economic structures and proceed accordingly.

20

Understand the specific value in everyone.

A colleague of mine told me, on several different occasions, that she was impressed by my compassion as a man for the special requests she made as a woman and mother over time at the law firm. These requests included working remotely before it was in vogue (and certainly before it was necessitated by COVID-19), having unusual flexibility with respect to scheduling meetings, and taking proactive efforts to have her work matters covered while she was on maternity leaves *and* promptly shifting matters back to her so she was appropriately busy once back from maternity leaves. All of these are the sort of things that every law firm claims to do, but very few actually do. From my colleague's perspective, my understanding of her needs was incomprehensible because I am a man. For me, however, understanding her specific situation was no different than understanding any other person's specific situation. Understanding a person's specific situation is critical to understanding the specific value in each person. And that is the point I want to make in this Chapter: it is extremely helpful to understand the specific value in everyone with whom you interact.

The notion that we are all unique is a concept that seems to get a lot lip service, but rarely pursued with any effort. My advice to you is to truly learn the way in which each of your colleagues has a unique set of concerns, abilities, skills, weaknesses, personality type, homelife, background and so on. Learning the way in which each person is unique is an ongoing process that takes patience and effort, but is well worth it. Knowing the ways in which each person is unique will enable you to identify the specific value in each person.

Knowing the specific value in each person was very beneficial to me in my career. You could say that knowing the specific value in each person gave me the compassion to help them grow in their own careers, and even lend an ear when they faced troubled times. Or you could say that knowing the specific value in each person gave me insights as to how best to extract value from such persons for my own gain. I believe in my heart that both statements are in fact accurate.

Two examples from my career might show how each statement above is accurate. One example is focused on an affable woman who did not have the skills needed in my practice area and the other example is focused on a man who did not have the disposition to bother with social graces, but was extraordinary at analyzing the complex economic formulae ubiquitous in private investment fund contracts (i.e., my practice area).

First, the affable woman. When we hired Charlotte, we felt good about our decision. She had a degree from a very good law school. She had two years of experience at another law firm, and we very much needed someone who could hit the ground running. She was warm and friendly in her interviews and clearly would work well with others on the team. Unfortunately, it was only a matter of months before it became clear that Charlotte did not possess the skills needed in my practice area, which meant that we would need to counsel her out (i.e., allow her time to find another job) to make room for someone with the skills we needed.

I was very worried about Charlotte, because I knew things did not look good for her long-term viability at our law firm. I was particularly worried about the impact to her confidence when it became clear to her that we wanted her to find a position elsewhere. I had a number of conversations with Charlotte about why we were asking her to find a position elsewhere, emphasizing that it was not a judgment about her worth as a person or skills as a lawyer, overall, but rather it was the harsh reality that we needed to open her position to find someone with the directly relevant experience we needed. Through these conversations, I discovered that she, like everyone, had extraordinary strengths. Her strengths lie outside my particular practice area and truthfully if the practice area in my law firm most suited to her strengths was hiring at the time, we would have transferred her internally.

While I and one or two other Partners made efforts to get to know what we could about Charlotte, in order to help her, others in my law firm started to ignore her. They knew she had no future with us at the law firm and presumably believed there was nothing to gain by getting to know Charlotte if she was soon leaving the firm. They were right about her future, but wrong in their approach. Knowing more about Charlotte made it possible to give her some guidance about where she might focus her career and it made me in good conscience willing to provide a strong recommendation to other law firms hiring, provided that they were hiring in an area of law for which she was well suited. Ultimately, Charlotte landed at another well-respected law firm, and within five or six years of leaving our firm, Charlotte made Partner at the other law firm.

My path crossed with Charlotte's both directly and indirectly over the years. My efforts to know her and willingness to help her avoided considerable consternation when the day came that a Client of mine was a personal friend of Charlotte's. I cannot say Charlotte ever forgave me for my role in counseling her out of our law firm, but I do believe she was reasonable and civil in the years thereafter because of the effort I made to understand her specific value. I know, for example, that my Client who was a good friend of Charlotte's would likely have not hired me if Charlotte had derogated my reputation.

Opposite from Charlotte, in almost every way, was Grumpy George. One of the most brilliant minds I have ever worked with was in the head of Grumpy George. Grumpy George understood mathematical realities of complex economic contracts almost instantaneously, while the rest of us would need many hours of analysis to really understand the verisimilitudes of such contracts. Notwithstanding his brilliance, many people shied away from working with Grumpy George, except when absolutely necessary. This is because Grumpy George was, you guessed it, very grumpy. Also, I believe he was perpetually annoyed at the stupidity of everyone else on earth. It seemed to irk him the most if one of his colleagues, the very people he had chosen to be grouped with, made any statement or came to any conclusion that was flawed. I think he felt that his own intelligence was insulted by association. Over time it occurred to me that his grumpiness was rooted in a deep desire that the world be a better place, that people think more clearly and more carefully, and that people try harder to find the answers to problems. People were constantly falling short of his hopes. The relentless pattern of hope and disappointment wore on him, manifesting in grumpiness (sometimes outright rudeness).

While others shied away from Grumpy George, I was fascinated by him. I wanted to know more about him, professionally and personally. I wanted to know why this guy was so grumpy all the time, and I very much wanted to learn from him given his preternatural ability to divine complex economic contract clauses. Truthfully, I thought to myself, this man is misunderstood. I can make his existence a tiny bit better by tolerating his grumpiness, and offering my friendship and kindness. And, I thought to myself, in the process I can include him on my matters, which will significantly improve the overall quality of legal services provided to my Clients, and I may even learn a thing a two. Sure enough, over time, I believe Grumpy George and I became friends. We worked together on the most complicated transactions and I can confirm to you that I learned an extraordinary amount from Grumpy George. Working with Grumpy George, I was able to complete transactions I would not have been able to complete without Grumpy George. And I believe in my heart that Grumpy George benefitted from my efforts to understand him as a person, relate to him, and offer him friendship.

In both the case of Charlotte and Grumpy George, my efforts to understand the specific values of each person enabled me to navigate difficult courses to much better destinations for all—them, me, the law firm and our Clients—than had I treated them as undifferentiated units of production and interacted (or avoided) them without knowledge of the specific values of each.

21

Focus on the 20 who like you.

This Chapter 21 covers the second-best business advice that I have ever received. It is a twist on an old secular parable.

Suppose you go into a room of 100 potential Clients. It is likely that 20 of them will be predisposed to like you, 20 of them will be predisposed not like you, and 60 will be somewhat neutral. Thus, with respect to 60 of the potential Clients, what you do matters a great deal in swaying them to either like you or not like you.

What should you do? Should you focus your energy on trying to change the minds of the 20 who are predisposed not to like you? Unfortunately, some people have a need to focus on this group. Some people simply cannot stand the fact that they are disliked by anyone, and when they meet people who are predisposed not to like them, they spend extra effort trying to prove to such group they should be liked. I hope it is obvious to you that this is not the group to focus upon.

Many advisers will tell you that you should focus on the 60 who are neutral towards you. After all, 20 of the potential Clients are already predisposed to like you. Why spend more energy on them when you could demonstrate to the neutral crowd that they should like you, and presumably sway some of them to like you.

Well, I'm here to tell you that you should focus on the 20 who like you and ignore the other 80. It is exactly what I did after I received this advice. The reason is simple. The world is huge.

There are nearly 8 billion people on the planet. 20% of 8 billion is one billion six hundred million. One billion six hundred million people is enough. Imagine one billion six hundred million people who are predisposed to like you. There is clearly no need to focus on those who are either predisposed not to like you or even those who are neutral. Spend your energy finding those that like you, and then focus exclusively on them.

Consider two examples.

Example 1: If you focus on the 60% who are neutral.

You go into the room I described above and you focus on the 60 who are neutral. With some effort, you convince one to become a Client. His name is Mr. Neutral. Mr. Neutral is happy when all is going well. Oops, you made a small mistake. Mistakes happen. Mr. Neutral is now wondering if he should have hired you. Picture in your mind a confidence meter that measures a Client's confidence in you. For Mr. Neutral the confidence meter points directly in the middle between zero confidence and 100% confidence. You do some good work and the meter moves a little towards 100% confidence. You make a mistake, however, and it plummets towards zero confidence. This is because humans have very strong loss aversion. Loss aversion is the phenomenon that humans hate negative events with far more intensity than they like positive events. One mistake for Mr. Neutral and you have dropped far below the starting point. Two mistakes, you are probably not going to work on Mr. Neutral's next legal matter. And, even if you only ever made the one mistake, Mr. Neutral is not likely to refer other potential Clients to you. He was neutral about you to start with and only because of your efforts to convince him to like you did he hire you. Once you make a single mistake, and the confidence meter plummets, he is not likely to put his own reputation on the line by referring others to you.

Example 2: If you focus on the 20% who like you.

Now imagine you went into the room I described above and focused on the 20 potential Clients who are predisposed to like you. It only makes sense that a greater number of them will agree to become your Client than if you focused on the neutral group. So, perhaps 5 of the 20 become Clients. For this example, we will look only at one of those Clients, Ms. Likesyou. Just as in Example 1, above, you do some good work for Ms. Likesyou. Her confidence meter started out well above neutral, because after all, she likes you. Then as you do good work the confidence meter really goes high. Oops, you made a mistake. The good news is that although the mistake brings your credibility measure down, you started from a higher level and so end up still above neutral. What's more, loss aversion applies only if a person perceives there to be a loss. When you make a mistake for Mr. Neutral, he perceives the mistake as a loss and it has a heavy toll on his confidence in you. When you make a mistake for Ms. Likesyou, she is far less likely to perceive it as a loss. After all, she likes you. It would be a challenge to her fundamental view of you to perceive the mistake as a great loss. Ms. Likesyou is probably going to chalk up the mistake to the vague and unavoidable imperfections of life. Even a second mistake is not likely to cause Ms. Likesyou to abandon you as her lawyer going forward. Because she likes you, she has unconsciously adopted you as her lawyer and she will not dump you unless and until there is a major blow-up between you. Another interesting difference between Ms. Likesyou and Mr. Neutral is that contrary to Mr. Neutral, who is unlikely to refer potential Clients to you, Ms. Likesyou is very likely to refer Clients to you as long as you do a good job on her legal matters. Clients who like you want to brag about their great lawyer to others, and the way they brag is to recommend you (with many flattering adjectives) to other potential Clients.

What I am trying to demonstrate in these little examples is that a person who likes you is more likely to hire you, more likely to stick with you and more likely to refer other Clients to you, simply because they like you. It's a trifecta of goodness. It's painfully obvious, isn't it, that you must focus on the 20% who like you? And because there are one billion six hundred million people on earth who are predisposed to like you, you do not have time to focus on everyone else. Okay, sure, not everyone on earth is looking for a lawyer, but even if you slice it down to those seeking the services you provide, I guarantee there is a sufficient population of potential Clients that you will never run out even if you focus only on the people who are predisposed to like you.

This advice applies to working relationships within the law firm, too. When you begin your legal career, you will not be able to choose the Partners for whom you work. But in a relatively short period of time, you will be able to demonstrate some preferences. Sometimes this can be achieved by constantly pursuing Partners you like for more and more work. Sometimes it must be done by speaking to a mentor or work coordinator about getting assigned more work from the Partners you like. Never forget to tell Partners you like working for that you like working for them. I loved hearing this; even when I was a Partner at one of the world's most prestigious law firms it was important to me to receive that kind of validation from my team. It's just human to want to hear you are doing a good job. This doesn't go away just because someone becomes an established Partner, an old man or old woman in the eyes of Junior Associates. Do not worry about sounding obsequious. A genuine compliment is never misunderstood for insincerity. Focus on the Partners who are predisposed to like you and you will have a much easier time being successful in your law firm.

22

Always perform at the level of the job you want, regardless of the level of the job you have.

If you are performing your job well, you have earned the ability to keep that job. Nothing more, nothing less.

Always perform at the level of the job you want, regardless off the level of the job you have. If you want a promotion, you must perform at the higher level. Your boss and others will see you performing at the higher level, see that you are performing as if promoted, and you will have removed any good reason not to be promoted.

A lot of people think that performing the basic requirements of the job they have should mean, after some time, that they are ready to be tested at the next level. In other words, these people believe that simply doing their job should eventually mean they get a promotion; as if doing their job gives them the *right* to a promotion after some period of time. This is very, very wrong. Doing your job means only that you have a good chance of keeping your job, and even that is not guaranteed.

The work world does not owe you anything. The work world does not know you exist, beyond those with whom you interact directly. The work world will grind on with or without you, just as it has for centuries. There are no "secret rules" in the work world. No promises. There is only what you do, and importantly, what people see you do. The only way to get promoted is to perform in a way that others see you as capable of performing at the next level up. Ergo, perform at the level of the job you want, regardless of the level of job that you have.

It was clear to me by my third-year practicing law that I would never enjoy being a lawyer at a law firm unless I became a Partner. I began to ask questions, from time to time, about what it takes to become a Partner. I also observed keenly to see what Partners were doing that Associates were not. I could not magically perform as a Partner at such an early stage of my career, but I could begin the process of learning everything I could about what it would take to be a Partner.

It took me eight years of practicing law at large law firms (I am not including nearly two years hiatus having a solo practice), before I made Partner. I know that I performed at the level of a Junior Partner for at least two years before actually getting the promotion. This didn't bother me at all, because I knew that one must first perform at the level of the job one wants before actually being promoted to such level. There are legions of discontented Senior Associates griping about the fact that they have not yet been promoted to Partner, and venting bitterly about all the Partner-level stuff they are doing. Nobody seems to have told them the basic rule set forth in this Chapter. It's too bad, because they would be happier if they knew that they were on the right track. They are not being wronged by a delay in promotion, rather their law firm is watching closely, vetting them before the momentous step of promoting them to partner. It is appropriate that they remain an Associate while they prove their ability to perform at Partner level.

I recall one Senior Associate at my law firm who performed very well as a Senior Associate and, in due time, began performing at the level of a Junior Partner. Things were going very well for him at the law firm and everyone knew that he would be promoted to Partner. But he almost derailed his own career by decrying the injustice of our law firm when he did not make Partner in the year he believed he deserved to make Partner. His outrage was clear in his words, his tonal qualities and even his body language. I can recall clearly the moment a Partner from the Promotions Committee came to my office to discuss the fact that if this particular Senior Associate continued to thrash about with disparaging remarks about the law firm and its Partners, he was almost certainly going to derail his chances of being promoted. It was a razor close situation, saved primarily by two Senior Partners who went well beyond the normal call of duty to meet with him and convince him that all was well. Their objective in meeting with this Senior Associate was to keep him from sabotaging his own promotion by assuring him that he would be promoted the following year. Although he remained convinced that a great injustice had been perpetrated against him (because he was required to wait a year longer to be promoted to Partner than he had expected), he did understand that with these two Senior Partners backing him in the promotions process he was better off quieting down. He was promoted to Partner the very next year. I would be willing to bet that he now views that one-year delay as nothing, really, in the grand scheme of things—after all, he is now and has been ever since, a Partner in a prestigious global law firm. I would also be willing to bet that what he once perceived as being *outrageous* he now understands as being *essential.* He, like all Partners who had come before him, needed to perform at the level of Partner for a couple of years before our law firm was confident that he should be promoted to Partner.

The fact that one must always perform at the level of the job one wants, regardless of the level of the job one has remained true even after I made Partner. Very soon after making Partner, I became curious about the role that Equity Partners[3] play at the law firm and so the pattern started all over again. I began sleuthing what I could about what the next level of Partner requires and I began as soon as I could to perform at the next level. It took me another five years to be promoted again, and I believe in my heart that I was performing at the next level for at least two of those five years. But I was content. I knew that to be promoted to the higher level of Partner, I must perform at such higher level first. And so, I did. And then, after being promoted to the next level of Partner, I was curious about what it took to run a practice area. I repeated the process, again seeking knowledge on how one is selected to lead a practice area and what skills are required; again, as I learned what is expected I began to performed at the level of the job I wanted. In due time, I was given the opportunity to be practice area leader, globally, for the Private Equity Funds Practice Area at Morgan Lewis.

Looking back, I see that the pattern repeated from my days as a Summer Associate all the way to my five-year tenure as the head of the Private Equity Funds Practice Area at Morgan Lewis. I knew at every level that the only way I was going to get promoted to the next level was to perform at the next level. I knew the only way to perform at the next level, was to learn all I could about what the next level requires. And now you know, too. You

3. My law firm had two tiers of Partners. The first tier was so-called "Income Partners" and the second tier was so-called "Equity Partners." The primary distinctions were that Income Partners had pre-determined incomes that did not vary with profits and limited voting power in the partnership while Equity Partners shared in profits which might go up or down from year to year and had full voting power in the partnership.

must always perform at the level of the job you want, regardless of the level of the job you have.

23

Nobody gets paid to play tag football.

I think I annoyed a number of Associates who worked for me by always reminding them that nobody gets paid to play tag football. Professional football players in the NFL get paid a lot of money. To make that money, they must be willing to be in the game and get beat around a bit. They must be willing to hit hard and be hit hard. If you are not willing to hit hard or be hit hard, then professional football is not for you. You might enjoy tag football better. But to my knowledge, nobody gets paid to play tag football.

When I say, "nobody gets paid to play tag football," it is meant to redirect Junior Associates who fall into a pattern of aversion. It happens more often than you might think. There are some amazing Junior Associates, with spectacular skills of research and persuasive writing, drafting contracts, analyzing complex issues of law and nearly every other aspect of being a lawyer. But the reality is that to practice law fully, beyond the basics of a first- or second-year Associate, one must negotiate fiercely with opposing lawyers, one must prepare legal work that is presented directly to Clients without being improved upon first by Partners, one must speak up to correct a colleague if one's colleague is in error. Direct confrontation is required to be a good lawyer. These activities are, by analogy, like the hard hits in professional football.

When you begin to engage in the hard-hitting aspects of being a lawyer, such as negotiating with opposing lawyers, interacting directly with Clients, speaking up to correct colleagues and so on, it is only natural that those being confronted by you will react confrontationally back. A lawyer opposing you will try to pick apart your position. A Client will criticize your work. Colleagues will defend vigorously their point of view as you try to correct them. Many times, this will all be happening in front of observers, which amplifies the sensation of the hard hits. Clients may be watching you negotiate with opposing counsel. Partners may be watching you interact with Clients. You may be in a crowded conference room when you find that you must speak up to correct a colleague, because waiting until you have a moment alone will be too late to protect the interests of a Client. I wish it were not true, but the verbal jousting can be brutal. Too much is on the line for everyone to be polite all the time.

As you can see, to fully develop as a lawyer you will need to learn how to both hit hard and stand up against hard hits, metaphorically. You must be willing to get in the game at a professional level. You must be willing to choose the hard-hitting reality of practicing law over some other career more akin to tag football, just as the professional football player chooses the hard-hitting world of the NFL.

There are a few naturally confrontational people, but most of us avoid confrontation by nature. We do not seek confrontation in our daily lives and we do not seek it professionally. Not many people go around looking to give or receive hard hits. But because I viewed the ability to be confrontational as a necessary skill to zealously represent my Clients, I learned over the years how to hit hard and take hard hits.

A note about confrontation: Confrontation requires nothing more than being assertive. A teacher of mine once explained to me the distinction between being assertive and being aggressive. Being assertive is presenting your position with confidence, demanding nothing more and nothing less than for your position to be understood and respected. Being aggressive is attacking another *person* (i.e., attacking a person rather than an issue, fact or point of law). When you are aggressive, you attack in a way that forces the other person to defend themselves. Often in common vernacular the word "aggressive" is used to mean "assertive" and so there is much confusion on the topic. Do not fret if you are told to be "aggressive," because it is very likely what you are being asked to be is "assertive." Keeping the concepts separate will enable you to be a much more effective lawyer.

You will be able to differentiate aggressive tactics from assertive tactics simply by whether or not the tactics involve personal slights and insults. Assertive tactics do not involve personal slights and insults, but rather rely entirely on knowledge and logic. Aggressive tactics do not rely on knowledge and logic, but rather depend heavily on the use of personal slights and insults.

Beware using aggressive tactics. It is very rarely the case that being aggressive has better results than being assertive. I believe it is the opposite, in fact. It is counterproductive to be vitriolic or abusive during the zealous representation of your Client. On occasion, I have seen perfectly good business transactions die because the lawyers could not resist all-out personal warfare with increasingly aggressive tactics, and in some of those circumstances, I have seen the lawyers fired by their Clients.

I have noticed that Associates who have between four and six years of experience often affect unnatural aggression during negotiations solely because they believe it is their duty to do so. This was just as true for me as for anyone else. One negotiation stands out in particular from my fourth year as an Associate. I was negotiating against another fourth-year associate at another law firm, who I am sure was also under the impression we were obligated to be as mean as possible to each other. Our telephone conversations would become shouting matches full of profanity. It was absurd. Thankfully, we never had to negotiate in front of our Clients or I am sure we would both have been fired by our respective Clients.

But you might ask, how do you reconcile the professional football analogy, on the one hand, with the notion that one should be assertive rather than aggressive, on the other hand? The analogy to professional football is better than you think. Contrary to popularly held beliefs, football is actually not about personal attacks on opposing players, but rather it is about one team making touchdowns and field goals, while keeping the other team from making touchdowns and field goals. That's all. The rest is strategy, and strategy will certainly include blocking and tackling—a lot of hard hits. But the hits are not *per se* personal attacks. Sure, players can become emotional and the hits can become personal. This is why there are nearly 300 pages of rules in the NFL Rulebook, all designed to keep a sport of hard hits from becoming life-threatening personal warfare. In the practice of law, we have Rules of Professional Conduct (ethics) in order to keep the practice of law from becoming personal warfare. Arguably the most significant ethical obligation we have as lawyers discourages us from engaging in personal attacks on opposing lawyers—i.e., our duty to zealously represent the interests of our Clients will rarely be compatible with attempts to attack opposing counsel personally.

The more you force yourself to be assertive, and resist the temptation to be aggressive, the better you become at it and the easier it becomes for you. The better you are at being assertive, the less you will be tempted to rely on being aggressive. So, like football (or any sport), the more you train at it, the better you will be at it.

"Nobody gets paid to play tag football" is good advice not just for those who have a natural aversion to confrontation. It is also good advice for those who are terrified to make a mistake. I have known during my career some brilliant lawyers who excelled in every way, but were terrified of making a mistake. Being told they made a mistake was, for them, worse even than confrontation. Mistakes were for them very hard hits indeed. And if a Client or opposing counsel pointed out a mistake it seemed to be an almost fatal blow to these lawyers.

It is only natural that some new lawyers will end up being this way as they enter law firms. After all, they may have been at the top of their class in high school and again in college. They clawed their way through law school and then the Bar Exam. Having the right answers, not making mistakes, was the one thing that assured them of success their entire lives. They have been fed a steady diet of external validation—praise for having the right answers and criticism for having the wrong answers. In such a system, there is very little incentive to develop a tolerance for risking mistakes. Unwittingly, some people come out of law school more akin to first-generation artificial intelligence than full-blown lawyers. They are comfortable doing the automaton-like tasks of research, analysis and writing. But nothing further. I want to emphasize that this has happened to some portion of every class of lawyers in the modern era—this is not a character trait of any particular generation, but rather a character trait found in a small percentage of every generation.

To those terrified to make a mistake I say, "nobody gets paid to play tag football."

So, when you are a little scared about upcoming negotiations, Client meetings or internal meetings with colleagues, whether because you fear confrontation or because you fear making mistakes, just remind yourself that such activities are at the heart of being a good lawyer. Remind yourself that you are paid handsomely for being in the game, exposed to hard hits and willing to make hard hits. Remind yourself that nobody gets paid to play tag football.

24

Your job is your choice, you are free to leave.

I include this obvious tidbit, because it was something I lost track of during my early years as a lawyer. I was sitting in a meeting with the full Corporate Practice Group at Pillsbury, Madison & Sutro LLP (now branded simply Pillsbury) and a Senior Partner was describing a deal he and I were working on together. I did not realize it at the time, but he was giving me a compliment by noting the complexity of the issues and esoteric nature of the laws in question. I made a sarcastic quip, meaning only to be humorous, to the effect that I was "lucky" to be learning an area of law almost sure to never come up again in my career. The comment received a round of laughter, but the Partner was offended. Looking back, I now understand, because I had in a sense rejected his kindness. He said to me and to the entire group, that we should never forget that everyone in the room was there at their own choosing. Everyone was free to leave at any time if the work didn't suit. I was startled by his stern reaction to my quip, but it dug a deep groove in my memory.

Over the years, I thought about his comment in many different situations. It was extremely helpful in the toughest times. The times when I was most exhausted or overwhelmed by the demands of the profession, I would recall the stern comment from that Partner. I would remind myself, "I am here at my own choosing and I am free to leave at any time."

When you point this out to yourself during a challenging time, you are forced to answer the immediately following question: "Why don't you leave?" If you spend even a minute or two really answering that question, it somehow lightens the intensity of the situation.

Years after the meeting at Pillsbury, Madison & Sutro I was in the middle of a large, complex transaction and requests were coming in from the Client and Partners faster than I could even respond to confirm that I would do as asked. Being under that kind of rapid fire is extremely stressful. I was frustrated and even getting angry and then it popped into my mind. I recalled the stern remark from the Partner. I thought, "I am here at my own choosing and I am free to leave at any time." I then asked myself if I wanted to leave, essentially to quit. My answer was "no" before I could really articulate the question. At first, I thought, "no, I have too much student debt." But I knew that answer was incomplete. The legal job market was robust at the time. I could switch jobs and still pay my student debt.

So, I thought about it more. I asked, again, "If I can switch jobs and still pay my student debt, why don't I quit? I am under extraordinary stress and the demands seem to be increasing rather than decreasing." The more I thought about it, the more I realized that I had developed a kind of negative myth around the work—i.e., that it was ever-increasing and overwhelming; never decreasing or sustainable. When I stopped to challenge my inner dialogue, I was forced to admit that I was experiencing only a temporary deluge of work, it would pass. Taking a wider perspective, I realized that I liked being at a well-known law firm representing Clients in significant transactions. Thus, I concluded: "For the time being, I choose to be here. I do not want to leave."

In each tough situation in which I recognized to myself that I chose to be there and did not want to leave, it removed all of the unpleasantness that came with viewing myself as stuck against my will. You may think it is odd for a Junior Associate to view himself as forced to be working at a law firm. After all, obtaining a position as an Associate at a law firm is achieving an enormous goal. But the feeling of being trapped comes when you are handling extraordinary amounts of work and struggling to meet Client and Partner demands. It can feel as if there is no choice in the situation, as if you have made a terrible decision by becoming a lawyer and now you are imprisoned forever by such choice.

Given the importance of how we feel in a situation, regardless of the objective truth of the situation, I believe it is important to have a tool that enables Associates to free themselves emotionally from feeling trapped. Reminding yourself from time to time that your job is voluntary and that you are free to leave is such a tool. Reminding yourself of all the reasons you remain an Associate at a law firm—knowing that you are there by choice and staying by choice—is very empowering.

25

Your boss is not your parent; your subordinate is not your child.

Because of the age difference between a Partner and a Junior Associate, it is easy to see why some Partners view their young Associates as if they were their children and some Junior Associates view Partners as if they were their Parents. This is fraught with danger on many fronts.

If a Partner has a bad relationship with his children, it is unfair for him to infuse any work relationship, consciously or subconsciously, with the negative emotional baggage of his homelife. A young Associate who already has enough to handle learning the practice of law should not carry an invisible burden of an acrid prejudice against him held by the Partner. It would be impossible for such Junior Associate to ever perform well in the eyes of such a prejudiced Partner.

If a Partner has a good relationship with her children, it is still not a good idea for her to view young Associates as if they were her own children. In this situation the dangers are different, but also damaging. Imagine a Partner who thinks her children can do no wrong and, more than anything, wants to preserve the good relationship she has with her children. If this Partner views a Junior Associate through such lens, it will very likely stunt the growth of the Junior Associate. Such growth will be stunted as a result of protection the Partner provides to the Junior Associate. This protection can range from saving the Junior Associate from the worst assignments to shielding the Junior Associate from harsh criticism from Clients or other lawyers. If the Junior Associate is not challenged with all the varied assignments other Junior Associates receive, he will not grow at the same rate. If the Junior Associate is protected from harsh criticism, he is harmed both by never knowing the areas he should improve and by never developing skills to cope with harsh criticism.

If a Junior Associate has a bad relationship with his parent(s), he is doomed if he attributes the negative emotional baggage from that relationship onto a Partner. Imagine how little the Junior Associate wants to help the Partner if the Junior Associate has consciously or subconsciously concluded the Partner is just like his parent. Imagine the potentially inappropriate statements he might make and inappropriate tonal qualities he might use when speaking to the Partner.

If a Junior Associate has a good relationship with her parent(s), it will still not benefit the Junior Associate to view a Partner as if a parent. The Junior Associate may let her guard down in ways she should not, perhaps by expecting the Partner to monitor her like a parent (see Chapter 15 *Nobody is monitoring you daily or weekly*) and protect her from undesired work assignments or overwhelming amounts of work. See Chapter 10 *Understand and respect your limits*. The Junior Associate may adopt an informal familial manner around such Partner that the Partner finds awkward and off-putting.

At my law firm, there was a young woman named Stephanie. Stephanie had a very complicated relationship with her father, and from what she shared with me it sounded as though her father was emotionally abusive. It was clear that while Stephanie loved her father, she did not *like* her father very much. Among other things, her father crushed her between (i) an expectation that Stephanie should be a successful lawyer and (ii) harsh criticism regardless of such success. Stephanie's father was a Partner at another large law firm. Her father pushed her into law school against her true desires and continued to put pressure on Stephanie even after she began to practice law.

Stephanie worked primarily for Peter Phleger, a Senior Partner who was universally beloved at my law firm. Peter was calm and fair in all situations; he was truly unflappable. He was also unwaveringly, sometimes painfully, honest. He was extraordinarily knowledgeable and a kind teacher, generous with his knowledge and his time. In all of my years practicing law, there was no better Partner to work for than Peter Phleger. I tell you this both because I really like Peter, but also to highlight the distortion that can occur if a young Associate subconsciously views a Partner as if he is her father.

It was not apparent immediately, but over time it became clear that Stephanie begrudged Peter at every assignment. It was clear that Stephanie just didn't want to help Peter. Stephanie would occasionally have inappropriate outbursts, exactly like a child angry at her father, decrying the unfairness of assignments and deadlines and all manner of complaints. The way Stephanie would sometimes speak to Peter, the tonal qualities alone, were so much like a disgruntled daughter speaking to a father that on occasion Peter was drawn into the mindset of father-daughter and would lecture her like a father might. It was an unproductive working relationship and Stephanie had everything to lose. Not long after an incident in which Stephanie had a temper tantrum, and went so far as to throw at Peter a document they were working on together, she was counseled out of the law firm.

You might say to yourself that the above information is interesting, but how is it helpful? How could anyone possibly prepare for, or defend against, the subconscious infiltration of parent-child dynamics into the Partner-Associate relationship? How does one defend against that which she is not conscious? My answer is to be on guard against it; bring the subconscious into the conscious; merely knowing such problems might exist shines the light of knowledge into the dark corner of ignorance. Knowing this problem can exist is 90% of the solution. Identifying and addressing the problem early is the remaining 10% of the solution. Addressing the problem, once identified, is as simple as the old adage, "Act like a professional and an adult, and you will be treated as a professional and adult."

Ask yourself, as you get to know a Partner through successive projects, does anything about the Partner remind you of any of your parents? If the answer is "yes," then immediately course correct and say to yourself, out loud if necessary:

> "[Name of Partner] is a very experienced lawyer who can teach me much about practicing law. [He/she] is not my [father/mother]. [He/she] is no more my [father/mother] than any other random human being on the face of the earth. My job is to work hard for [Name of Partner] and [his/her] job is to lead professionally. Nothing more; nothing less."

If you are being treated as if a child, you might need to be assertive and explain politely to the Partner that you are an adult, a professional and a member of the Bar. You might explain that although you are grateful for the Partner's desire to be so kind as to provide a broader spectrum of advice than merely advice related to the practice of law, in your case the Partner need not spend extra time or effort on topics unrelated to the practice of law. You might add that you have a network of mentors outside the specific projects you are doing for such Partner.

It is paramount that in any conversation with a Partner in which you seek to redirect the Partner away from a child-parent dynamic, you must communicate in a way that makes the Partner feel appreciated and respected. See Chapter 5 *The best business advice I ever received.* It will be important to choose the right moment to bring up the topic with a Partner, such as when a Partner begins to give you unsolicited advice about an aspect of your life unrelated to the specific projects you are working on with the Partner. If you raise the issue at the right time and communicate in a polite way, I am confident you will find that Partners seeking the parent-child dynamic will shift their focus to other Associates who are more willing to be mothered or fathered; your career will progress unmarred. I suspect you will, in fact, be perceived with great respect by paternalistic and maternalistic Partners as being very mature, beyond the need of their fathering and mothering. And all others at your law firm will have increased respect for you, too, after they see you deftly handle the situation.

26

A problem is only as dire as your reaction.

Not to brag, but I am famous for the particular skill I am sharing with you in this Chapter 26. I am not certain where I learned it, but I suspect it was during my rambunctious childhood. I was never a bad person, but I had a lot of energy and things I did would often end up somehow outside the rules. Over the years of giving explanation after explanation as to what had happened, how it had happened and why it had happened, I began to see a very curious pattern. I began to notice that the wrath of the adult, be it a parent, a teacher, a sports coach, whomever, was correlated with the nature of my response in the face of the transgression. Truly, the degree and nature of the response from the adult seemed influenced in some manner by my response to them in the heat of the situation.

What I mean specifically is that if I gave the impression that I had done an awful thing, the adult followed the same emotional reaction and meted out punishment for said awful thing. But if I reacted as though it were really not such an awful thing, with assurances as to how it would be remedied, then adults tended to follow that emotional guide and mete out punishment, if any, accordingly. Often there was no additional punishment beyond the remedy I had devised for them already. The trick, if it is a trick, is to not deny the wrongful act but rather be ahead of the adult emotionally in having a response to it.

For example, suppose as a teenager I broke a vase in my house.

Consider how events might have unfolded if I did not utilize my ability to emotionally lead. I might have sat in fear for hours after breaking a vase, anticipating my mother's anger and disappointment when she came home. Such fear may have motivated me to devise a plan to avoid the consequences of breaking the vase. I might have tried to hide the broken vase or I might have denied being the one who broke the vase. In each scenario, my mother's reaction would have been harsh. Imagine her anger and disappointment when she realized the vase was gone, that I had broken it and that I had hidden the evidence. Or, imagine her anger and disappointment if, upon arriving home to see a broken vase, I began to tell lies about having not broken the vase. My reactions would have set the stage for her to be very angry and disappointed.

Now, consider how events might have unfolded if I used my ability to emotionally lead. When my mother arrived home, I would tell her I broke the vase and that I knew how to replace it from my allowance. I would communicate in an even-keeled voice and unemotional state. What could she do? The most natural reaction would be to tell me to be more careful and, yes, replace the vase.

Over time I realized that there is an ability to emotionally lead others, and I learned it applies in many situations. To be sure, it is more of an art than a science. It is imperfect in its application. But it worked reasonably well as a child and it worked extraordinarily well as a lawyer. Representing Clients is a marvelous place to utilize the art of emotionally leading others, as I will explain below.

Fast forward from my childhood to my legal career and I can categorize the situations during my career in which I utilized the art of emotionally leading others into (i) those situations involving a mistake made by me or my team and (ii) those situations involving a negative set of facts and circumstances—i.e., hard luck—for my Clients.

Emotional Leading After a Mistake

When a mistake happens, and they will happen, being prepared with a solution and an emotional state that conveys "all is (or will be) fine" leads to a much calmer reaction from Clients than if you react in a panicked or very concerned manner. If you panic, your Client will follow suit. Your panic will trigger their panic. Your concern will trigger their concern. And once the Client is panicked or concerned, what naturally follows is anger. And the kind of anger Clients unleash on lawyers who make mistakes, after spending hefty amounts of money for top notch legal services, can be a very unpleasant anger to receive.

It is critical that you understand that you must acknowledge the mistake; denying it or hiding it will undermine your credibility (and is also an ethics violation). Credibility is the key component to emotionally leading others. Without credibility, no sane person would follow your emotional lead after a mistake.

I recall a situation at one of my former law firms in which a state securities law filing was required in connection with the offer and sale of limited partner interests in a private equity fund, and a simple mistake led to a $10 million fee for the Client. The state law had a filing fee of $0.01 per share issued. It is important to note that the filing fee was based on the number of "shares" issued, and not the value of those shares. The private equity fund was raising $1 billion dollars. A private equity fund is extremely unlikely to be publicly traded and there is very little reason for it to have a large number of shares, regardless of how large the dollar amount in question. In fact, the concept of "shares" is a corporation concept and does not fit a partnership structure, and P.E. funds are very often structured as limited partnerships. Nonetheless, the law required stating a number of shares and so it would have been normal for the securities law filing to show somewhere between 1 and 100 shares. The filing fee would thus have been between $0.01 and $1 (which would then result in a statutory minimum fee of $500). Unfortunately, someone without proper experience in such filings in the context of a private equity fund assumed (it's always dangerous to assume!) that the number of shares should match the dollar amount on a 1:1 basis. This meant that the filing stated total shares issued of 1,000,000,000. A month later the Client received a computer-generated notice in the mail indicating that $10 million was due as the filing fee.

As you might imagine, the Client called and was extremely alarmed. The Client was frantic, explaining that, "the fee would wipe out the first $10 million of profit for the private equity fund and law suits would start flying and, oh my God, might they go to jail or something?" Furthermore, the careers of all involved at the private equity fund would be over for good, because their reputations would all be ruined.

My friend at the law firm who was the Partner responsible for this Client had adopted my approach of emotional leadership. (He was kind enough to give me credit for the technique, in fact.) His response with the Client was first to assure them that they would not be paying a $10 million securities law filing fee. He then promptly admitted the mistake and explained what happened and what should have happened. Finally, he assured them that he would solve the situation and they needn't worry about a thing. After all, it was merely a clerical error at our firm that led to a computer-generated filing fee invoice for the incorrect amount. In the end, my friend was able to coordinate with the Secretary of State and supervise an amended filing showing only a small number of shares issued and resulting in the Client paying only the statutory minimum fee of $500. In the end, my friend emotionally led the Client to view the entire snafu as a humorous anecdote.

Emotional Leading in Hard Luck

Many leaders in the legal profession talk about the goal of being a "trusted adviser" to your Clients. This is a key goal, no doubt about it. But I come at this topic from a slightly different angle than many others. My view is that the most valuable use of being a trusted adviser, and the skill that is most likely to get you to be a trusted adviser, is to be able to emotionally lead Clients.

Lawyers are often called when things are not going well for Clients. Perhaps a Client is being sued or they need to sue someone else for a wrong done to them. Perhaps they wish to embark on a significant business transaction full of uncertainty and risk. Perhaps they are going bankrupt. Perhaps they received a nasty letter from the IRS or the SEC or any number of other regulators. A seemingly endless list of bad situations, which collectively I will call "hard luck" can befall any person and any company. Lawyers are here to help Clients through such hard luck.

It is this aspect of the role of lawyers in society, being there for Clients during their times of hard luck, that has, over the centuries, resulted in a conflation of hard luck times and the lawyers who are there to help. The coterminous nature of hard luck and interacting with lawyers has, over time, led to a vague sense in the public at large that lawyers are somehow responsible for the hard luck or, at a minimum, should be criticized for profiting from the hard luck of others. But the logic is flawed. We lawyers obviously do not create the hard luck. Furthermore, no lawyer I ever met loved her work so much that she would do it for free. Quite the opposite. It is a demanding profession and without the pecuniary rewards there would be no lawyers to help Clients through such Clients' hard luck. But because this conflation of lawyers and hard luck times exists in the collective conscience of society, the use of emotional leading can gain you tremendous Client loyalty and admiration.

Suppose a Client calls you and is very concerned, nearly panicked about a situation. You could either (i) agree that the situation is awful and thereby confirm that their panic is exactly the right emotional state or (ii) keep calm, ask a few questions to make sure you understand the situation and then begin to explain why it is something well within your abilities to handle. As the Client hears that you can handle it, they are no longer overwhelmed by the fact that they cannot handle it. Your emotional state of "all is going to be well" becomes their emotional state. The Client is relieved, and if you have ever experienced panic, you know how wonderful subsequent relief feels. If you were not already their trusted adviser, you are now. They may still view lawyers, generally, as somehow responsible for the world's hard luck, but they will blame all of the *other* lawyers. You will hold the special place in their mind as the good lawyer, the kind of lawyer all lawyers should be: The Trusted Adviser.

Why Emotionally Leading Works for Lawyers

I found during my legal career that emotionally leading Clients as an adult and lawyer was far easier than emotionally leading parents, teachers and sports coaches in my childhood. I found this to be a paradox, because my Clients' matters were vastly more important than any mischief I might have found as a child.

But it eventually dawned on me that it all comes down to credibility. For better or for worse, as a child you do not have much credibility with adults. Parents, teachers and sports coaches are all preconditioned to question the accuracy and veracity of statements from children. But when it comes to the attorney-Client relationship, it is very different.

Clients are preconditioned to rely upon the accuracy and veracity of statements from their lawyers. You might say this is because lawyers have a fiduciary duty to zealously represent Clients' interests, but perhaps it is also because the subject matter involved is often far afield of Clients' areas of expertise. How would they know which emotional response is appropriate for a situation that they do not understand?

Thus, if a mistake is made but you have a proposed solution and convey an "all is well" emotional state, they see you as a problem solver and they naturally adopt your "all is well" emotional state. Similarly, if a situation develops such that a Client is in hard luck, but your reaction is "all will be well" and you begin establishing a game plan for moving forward, the Client will shift their emotional state from panic or concern to "all will be well" and follow your lead on the action plan for moving forward.

27

Never lie. Never blame.

Never Lie.

The moment before you tell a lie is an interesting moment in time, a kind of critical junction or inflection point. Your future will hold many different possibilities at that moment. If you avoid the temptation to lie, your life progresses on a relatively predictable path. But once you decide to tell a lie, it is as if your life is going into a portal of distortion and there is no ability to know in which direction it will head.

The reason telling lies creates distortion is that once the untruth has been unleashed into the world, you impact other people who do not have the benefit you have of knowing the difference between the truth and the lie you have told. The unintended consequences of a lie are immeasurable; at a minimum you have done damage to yourself in an absolute sense. It is likely that you also have done damage to yourself in a relative sense vis-à-vis your reputation in the eyes of others.

The damage you have done to yourself in an absolute sense is immediate and unavoidable. When you lie, your aggregate worth—the sum total of your goodness—is reduced. The amount it is reduced is proportionate to the nature of the lie you have told, but even the smallest lie will chip away at your goodness. Consider in your mind someone you know who you believe very rarely lies. And now consider in your mind someone you know who you believe often tells lies. Is it not immediately clear in your mind which person is inherently better? If you go from being a person who rarely tells lies to a person who frequently tells lies, your goodness will degrade and it will impact every aspect of your life. Fortunately, the reverse is true, too, so you can always begin to rebuild your character, rebuild your aggregate goodness. But beware, while it only takes a single instant to ruin your reputation, it takes a very long time and extraordinary effort to rebuild your reputation once ruined.

With respect to your professional success, the damage you do to yourself in respect of your aggregate goodness will immediately change the way you seem to others. Your entire persona shifts a little with each lie, and the degree of the shift corresponds to the magnitude of your lies and the frequency of your lies. We have all met people in our professional lives who have become so accustomed to lying and have been lying for so long that their persona is almost entirely that of being a liar. Most often they believe they are fooling everyone, but in fact they stand out painfully as untrustworthy. These are the types of people described as "slimy" or "creepy" or other similar adjectives, even by people meeting them for the first time. Liars just ooze dishonesty.

Very few people will want to hire you if they believe you are dishonest. Very few people want to take the chance that you will be dishonest with them and others regarding their legal matters and, of course, your legal fees. Every time you tell a lie you shift a tiny bit towards the slimy and the creepy, building an aura around yourself of untrustworthiness.

Trustworthiness is the most delicate of all character traits. A bad act, a lie, repeated acts of selfishness are just a few ways that trustworthiness can be destroyed. Most people know not to trust untrustworthy people. You are deeply damaging yourself if you give anyone reasons not to trust you. If you are viewed as untrustworthy, you will be cut off from people and cut off from career opportunities. An untrustworthy person is an island far from the shores of humanity. When you lie to someone, you are telling them you are untrustworthy.

An unintended consequence of lying that is worth calling out in this book, because it is rarely discussed, relates to the fact that the person to whom you are lying may be able to tell you are lying as you are lying. If this is the case, then that person will either pretend not to know you are lying, in essence lying back to you, or will be forced to confront you on your lie. Most people do not enjoy being put in this situation. One of my bosses—a Senior Partner in one of the law firms where I worked—frequently lied to others in the firm about his role vis-à-vis important Clients and other matters of firm politics. Often, he would attempt to distort his lies into truth by repeating his version of reality to me and looking for me to confirm it. He was career gaslighting me, and I knew it while it was happening. I was very uncomfortable knowing he was lying and felt even worse about not speaking up. I wish I had the strength at the time to confront him from the very first lie, but the power dynamics between us were such that it would have risked my career to confront him. Instead, I pretended I didn't realize he was lying and I would say something vague in response, such as "okay," and then quickly change the subject. I started to feel that my role as a passive accomplice in his deceit chipped away at my character, and eventually I decided to leave that firm.

I had another boss, a Senior Partner in the San Francisco office of Morgan Lewis where I spent most of my career, who rarely told lies. The truthful boss was my favorite boss, and in fact he was everyone's favorite boss. I felt safe and comfortable working with the truthful boss, because I knew he was never going to burden me with the choice of participating in a lie or confronting him about a lie. There would be predictability in our dealings with each other, without the distorting effects of lies. I also knew that there would be predictability in our dealings with others, because lying simply wouldn't be involved in any manner. I learned over time working with the truthful boss that the universe of people surrounding him were all the type of people who gravitated towards honesty.

One day my truthful boss was late to an important conference call. Leaders at the highest levels at one of our corporate Clients were all waiting on the phone, as was I. These people were not the kind of people who liked to be kept waiting. Generally speaking, these people were extremely intelligent, very hard working, diligent and punctual and they expected all of these qualities from everyone else. Finally, my truthful boss joined the call and announced his presence. There was an awkward pause, and I could tell that my truthful boss must have realized that he had annoyed the leadership of our Client. I should note here that this Client was, in fact, my truthful boss's most important Client—the Client accounted for more than 80% of the total revenues attributed to my truthful boss. I waited silently and was very curious to hear what my truthful boss would say about being late. To my total joy and surprise, he said, "I'm sorry to be late, I couldn't find my wallet." I think everyone on the call was expecting some kind of an excuse, but nobody was expecting such prosaic honesty. On the one hand, it seemed outrageous that he would keep a gathering of important people waiting while he searched for his wallet, but on the other hand the sincerity of his statement and absolute lack of deception, the fact that telling some kind of "white lie" never even occurred to him, turned out to be a monumental occasion for his career. I found it charming. The General Counsel of our Client found it invaluable. The General Counsel was forever bonded to my truthful boss, and looked to my truthful boss as a trusted adviser forever thereafter. All of the most significant and sensitive issues were entrusted with my truthful boss. I cannot say the entire relationship was built on that one moment, it is more accurate to describe the relationship as having been built on dozens of such moments. But that was one of the more memorable moments, for me and for the Client.

You have probably heard the saying that "birds of a feather flock together." This is precisely the case in the professional world. The types of colleagues and Clients you will attract will be similar in character—similar in aggregate goodness—to yourself. Perhaps this is the reward for those who choose to be honest and forthright in their dealings with others and perhaps it is also the punishment for those who are deceptive.

Never Blame.

Blaming others, even when others make mistakes, is almost as bad for you as lying. The difference is that blaming others does not jeopardize your inherent goodness, unless you are lying when you blame someone else in which case see the discussion above about the deleterious effects of lying.

The reason you should never blame others is that it is more likely to undermine your credibility than actually shift accountability. In any professional situation you are either accountable for an outcome or you are not accountable, and this simply does not change regardless of who might have made a mistake along the way. If you are accountable for an outcome and the outcome was not achieved, you remain accountable. Blaming someone else for a mistake they made does not ameliorate the fact that the outcome was not achieved or the fact that you are accountable for such failure. It does not matter if someone else's mistake is truly the reason the outcome was not achieved, what matters is that you are accountable. Blaming others is nothing more than an attempt to shift accountability after learning a desired outcome has not been achieved. Everyone will see this as weak in character, because they will know you would not try to shift accountability if the desired outcome had been achieved.

There is an old expression, "Never explain, because your friends don't need it and your enemies won't believe you." This is equally applicable to blaming others for any failure to achieve an outcome for which you are accountable.

Blaming has another interesting side effect. It diminishes your esteem. If a Client looks to you as the person at your law firm who is accountable for a particular outcome, then they hold you in high esteem. If, upon failure to achieve the outcome, what they hear from you is blame pointed towards another person at your firm, they will realize that they should not have held you in high esteem; after all, the fate of the project was not controlled by you but rather it was controlled by such other person. Perhaps they should have been dealing with the other person all along? And if such other person was under your authority, then all you have achieved by blaming is to show that you are not skilled at leading others. Again, this diminishes your esteem in the Client's eyes. In fact, blaming subordinates is the worst kind of blaming.

Blaming anyone is ineffective, as discussed above, but it is most harmful to your reputation if you blame your subordinates. If you cannot accept responsibility, without blaming others, for a failure within your sphere of accountability, and instead try to blame the very people who you are leading, it will be clear to all that you lack the strength to be a leader. This causes serious damage to your reputation if you hope to build a stable of Clients or rise in the law firm to Partner or other leadership positions.

I recall a Partner at one of the law firms where I worked who was on a telephone call with a Client when I walked into her office. We had an appointment scheduled for that time. I didn't realize she was on a call, and her back was turned towards the door. She didn't see me and didn't realize I heard her say, "Well, I don't know, I keep telling Ted not to do that and he keeps screwing it up." I knew Ted was an Associate that worked for this Partner and so I thought she must be talking to another Partner at the law firm. I tapped lightly on her desk to let her know I was there. She turned to me, looked a little surprised and then said into the phone, "Melissa, I've got to go. Paul just walked in and we have a meeting. Is it okay if I call you back in half an hour?" I was stunned, because I knew Melissa was the General Counsel at one of our firm's Clients. I had never heard any Partner so bluntly blame an Associate to a Client. I asked, "what was that about?" The Partner said, "Ted keeps sending over documents with mistakes." In my head I thought, "well, Ted is only a second-year Associate and you are a Partner; it's your job to review Ted's work and make sure whatever goes to the Client is done right. But geez, even if you are too lazy to review his work you should at least have the constitution to be accountable for the quality of the work from your team." This wasn't the first time this Partner had used blame to try and deflect accountability. I immediately knew her blaming Ted was disingenuous. I am sure our Client did, too. It was no surprise that this Partner struggled to build her law practice.

I wish I could say that nobody who lies is able to be successful at a law firm. I wish I could say that nobody who blames others is able to be successful at a law firm. I cannot say either of those things. But what I can say is that from my experience practicing law at law firms from the 1990s until 2020 is that those who lie or blame must work many times harder to be successful than those who do not lie or blame. The liars and blamers are constantly navigating distortions of their own creating; constantly maneuvering and manipulating and building legion of people who think lowly of them throughout their careers. And at the end of such careers, they find they have nothing left of themselves, being of very little goodness by then, and they have no one in their world that trusts them or whom they trust. All in their world, whether it be family, friends or Clients are of equally little goodness. These are the Partners in a law firm who seem to shrivel into bitter curmudgeons, even while making fistfuls of money. Do not be fooled by the fistfuls of money, lying and blaming is a long and torturous path to emptiness and despair.

Telling the truth and accepting accountability pave a long and rewarding path to fulfilment and happiness, and you need not sacrifice one penny of profit on such path. Partners on this path are the Partners in a law firm who always seem to shine and bloom.

28

You are important, but so is everybody else.

It seems the more accomplished a Junior Associate is when entering the profession of law, the more likely they are to consider themselves important in an absolute sense. Remember that your accomplishments are relative, not absolute. If you were valedictorian, it simply means that you were a better student than other students in your class at your school. It says nothing about your capabilities as measured against students throughout the world, and much more importantly it says nothing about your capabilities against the vast number of experienced lawyers you are joining in the practice of law.

There are many ways in which some, certainly not all, Junior Associates enter the professional with an overestimation of themselves. Sometimes this results from an unbroken chain of academic accomplishments; sometimes from having lived in privilege with a vague sense of being better than everyone else; sometimes from athletic prowess; sometimes beauty; and sometimes from antipoles of these concepts—I have seen chips on the shoulders of Junior Associates who perceive themselves as having scratched their way out of poor neighborhoods and forgotten towns into the big leagues of a law firm believing they were better than the soft-skinned blue bloods surrounding them at the office.

Speaking of soft-skinned blue bloods, I recall one humorous evening at a firm social event. It was a charity fundraiser. My firm set up a mock casino whereby people could make a charitable donation of real money and acquire casino-styled chips to play various games as if in a real casino. Whoever had the most pretend value of chips at the end of the evening won a prize, which had also been donated for the charitable event. Before the mock gambling began, however, the evening started with a dinner and speeches about the charity. The dinner was organized in a large room with round tables, each seating about ten people.

I was a Senior Associate at the time and was seated at a table with several Partners, their spouses and a first-year Associate. It is natural for a first-year Associate who has been isolated from other Junior Associates to feel somewhat intimidated at a table with Partners and a Senior Associate. My nature is to be kind and inclusive in conversation if I see that someone else might be having a hard time. I was taught that good manners are nothing more than a desire to make everyone feel comfortable. But to my astonishment, the first-year Associate was not uncomfortable at all. The brash Junior Associate interjected, more or less interrupting conversation that was flowing among the Partners, to add what she believed to be very important anecdotes. Her perception of the importance of her anecdotes, it seemed to me, reflected her confidence that she was important. Being important herself, it seemed, meant that she was rightfully part of the conversation on equal footing with the Partners.

You might say, why not? Why shouldn't a first-year Associate feel confident to join into a conversation among Partners? After all, was she supposed to sit there quietly and submissively? Ah, well, let me finish the story. You see the problem was not that she participated in the conversation. The problem was not, even, that she, as a first-year Associate, participated with an air of importance and equality with Partners. The problem was that she was oblivious to the fact that her interjections were painfully off topic. Her obliviousness of the topic resulted from an arrogant overestimation of herself and underestimation of the others at the table in relation to herself.

The topic of conversation related to a legal development in the business industry of one of our Clients, and specifically about a new opinion that had been issued from the Supreme Court of the United States of America that was going to significantly impact such industry. While I was listening to see what I could learn from the Partners' discussion of the industry and the related laws, listening in a way that could be described as quiet and submissive, the first-year Associate decided to tell a story about her father's business. Unfortunately, her father's business was not in the relevant industry and the story seemed to have no nexus to the conversation. Even more cringeworthy, she insisted upon belaboring the story even as the Partners tried to politely move forward with the conversation. It was as if Marie Antoinette herself were interjecting an irrelevant anecdote into an otherwise learned discussion and expecting her subjects to transmute the anecdote into something relevant. In a single conversation, at a single dinner during a single law firm event, this young Associate made a lasting impression as an immature aristocratic nuisance in front of a table full of Partners.

In the following days, the Partners shared the story of this dinner as a humorous anecdote to other Partners and pretty soon this first-year Associate had a reputation as a prima donna. This alone is embarrassing, perhaps, but it is also a significant blow to a career. No Partner who seeks to assign work on an important case is going to risk giving the assignment to young Marie Antionette. And it did, in fact, come to pass that she was famously unhelpful on cases. Her snobbishness was a repellent against well-meaning colleagues and high-quality assignments. After approximately 18 months of never quite finding a rhythm with others, she left the law firm. My hope is that she started fresh, with an improved attitude somewhere else. I do not know. I never heard news of her, thereafter.

I remember thinking to myself at the moment of that dinner at that firm event, this first-year Associate thinks she is very important and simultaneously is somehow unaware of how important the others are at this table. That is when it hit me: *you are important, but so is everybody else.*

I am not recommending that Junior Associates view themselves as somehow unimportant. To the contrary, a Junior Associate is important in many ways. But the importance of a Junior Associate must be understood as a relative concept, not an absolute. In some circles and some situations, the Junior Associate is important. Perhaps she is responsible for running to ground dozens of facts critical to a case. Perhaps she is responsible for researching all relevant law for an important legal brief. There are myriad ways in which a Junior Associate is important. I want Junior Associates to be appropriately confident in their status and abilities. But, never ever forget that everyone else is important, too. Everyone.

To keep your ego in check, and avoid a cascade of events leading to your early demise at a law firm, you need only say to yourself, "I am important, but so is everybody else."

29

No task is beneath your status.

After doing well in high school, college, law school and passing the Bar Exam it might be easy for you to believe that you, as a lawyer, are not going to have to do menial tasks. And now I must be the cold splash of water in your face.

The vast majority of tasks assigned to a first-year lawyer are menial. You might be asked to proof read very lengthy documents, taking you days to complete, and then asked to proof read new copies of the same documents again when it turns out that such documents have been further revised while you were busy proof reading the first drafts. You might be asked to manually search for certain key terms occurring hundreds of times in hard-copy documents or scan thousands of emails for conversations between specific people discussing specific topics. You might be put in charge of organizing a room full of old documents, which are not available in electronic form, for the discovery phase of litigation. You might be pulled into legal due diligence for a corporate merger, which might require you to analyze dozens of contracts in search of anything that could impair the value of the target company. You might be asked to review thousands of pages of telephone calls and create a log of those between certain individuals. You might be asked to create a spreadsheet listing every shareholder of a company, the number of shares they purchased and whether or not they have signed "lock-up" agreements, which you would ascertain from review of thousands of corporate documents. These examples are real examples of work I was asked to do as a first year Associate, except for the example about reviewing telephone calls, that is from a scene in the movie *Clueless* that I found to be an accurate portrayal of legal work.

I remember thinking when I was a first year Associate that nearly anyone with an average IQ or higher could do the tasks I was given. My college degree was not relevant to completing such tasks. My law degree was not relevant to completing such tasks. What was relevant was my ability to see into the future; to understand that the menial tasks I was given were in fact components of incredibly complex projects being handled by our law firm; to have confidence that over time I would lead such projects; to realize that menial tasks would give me an opportunity to learn about the overall projects while having little risk of making mistakes that could ruin the outcome of such projects. My recommendation to you, of course, is to adopt these same views about any tasks you are given as a Junior Associate.

Many new lawyers do not understand the bigger picture and make the mistake of resisting or refusing menial tasks. There are three classic erroneous thoughts that lead a Junior Associate to conclude a task is beneath him:

1. Erroneous Thought One: I didn't become a lawyer to do the work of the uneducated masses.
2. Erroneous Thought Two: A Client shouldn't have to pay my hourly rate for this work.
3. Erroneous Thought Three: I won't learn anything from this assignment.

Erroneous Thought One does not need much analysis to understand why it is flawed. It is pretty straightforward snobbishness, an easily understood negative character trait.

Unlike Erroneous Thought One, which is rooted in snobbishness, Erroneous Thought Two and Erroneous Thought Three are not rooted in any negative character trait. It is not a negative character trait to want assignments that are fair and appropriate for the hourly rate charged to Clients by your law firm for your time. Nor is it a negative character trait to want assignments substantively appropriate to your education, so that you might continue to learn and grow. The flaw in both is rooted, however, in the limited field of view of Junior Associates.

In respect of those who believe there to be some economic injustice for charging high hourly rates for menial tasks (i.e., Erroneous Thought Two), they do not realize that significant amounts of their time are not ultimately charged to the Clients, at least not in the direct, linear manner new lawyers might assume. The time charges to a Client are managed by a Partner as part of an intricate balancing act of many variables, all as agreed between the Partner (or the law firm, as a whole) and a Client. For example, Partners might enter into arrangements with Clients that provide for blended fee rates across a team of lawyers of different levels of experience. Partners sometimes write off entire chunks of time recorded by junior lawyers or take other steps to accommodate Clients for the fact that Junior Associates will be doing menial tasks. The point being that there are many ways that law firm economics and Partner-Client relationships are managed to reach agreements that work for both the law firm and the Clients. A Junior Associate should never assume he knows how specific Partner-Client relationships work and then, on such basis, make a decision as to which assignments are appropriate for him and which are beneath his status as a lawyer. It is best to understand from the first day of your career that no assignment is beneath your status as a lawyer.

In respect of those who believe that they should resist assignments that do not require them to utilize their education or that do not teach them something substantive (i.e., Erroneous Thought Three), such Junior Associates do not realize that the Partners have a tremendous amount of experience training Junior Associates. Partners have a purpose to the sequencing of assignments throughout the beginning years of a lawyer's career, all as part of developing a powerfully effective lawyer. A Junior Associate should never assume he knows which assignments will benefit him best in his development as a lawyer and then, on such basis, make a decision as to which assignments are appropriate and which are beneath his status as a lawyer. It is best to understand from the first day of your career that no assignment is beneath your status as a lawyer.

Turning now to the consequences of deciding that certain assignments are beneath your status as a lawyer. The consequences relate directly to your most important asset as a lawyer: your reputation. You risk a reputation of arrogance or selfishness, because you will be viewed as having an unwillingness to do what it takes for the entire team to succeed. Note that your reputation is at risk regardless of why you resist or refuse menial tasks, because others do not know why you refuse or resist work, they will only know that you do.

An Associate who is perceived as unwilling to do what it takes for the entire team to succeed is unlikely to be invited to join teams. Meanwhile, an Associate who is perceived as willing to do what it takes for the entire team to succeed will be sought after by every team. After one or two years, the lawyer who realizes no task is beneath his status as a lawyer will be succeeding at the law firm, while the lawyer who believes (erroneously) that certain tasks are beneath his status will have stagnated in his development within the law firm or be gone from the law firm entirely.

To survive and succeed at a law firm, you must understand that no task is beneath your status as a lawyer.

30

Choose the business development approach that suits you best.

I was never any good at networking in the traditional sense. I find dinners and cocktail receptions very challenging. I never know what to talk about and find myself standing around awkwardly, often milling around near the bar or coffee station.

You might conclude based on the paragraph above that my career was not built on networking. You are correct. But this does not mean that I was not good at business development. Too many people conflate the two concepts and, unfortunately, come to the conclusion that if they are not naturally drawn to networking in the traditional sense then they are not good at business development. This leads to two possible unpleasant paths forward.

On one path, they abandon business development altogether. This means they never develop their own Clients and rely on providing services to the Clients of other lawyers at the law firm.

On the other path, many people decide to push forward with networking events as a necessary evil, even knowing that they have no inclination for the format, because they believe that networking is synonymous with business development. To make things worse, this group of people actually make networking events more painful for people like me, because they are very mechanical in their networking style, often trying to build conversation through an oral recitation of their curriculum vitae, which tends to reinforce my view that large-format, traditional networking events are tedious and dull.

Thankfully, you need not focus on large-format, traditional networking events if they don't suit you, because there are many different approaches to business development and surely one or more will suit you. Any of the approaches one might use to develop business is likely to be successful, provided that you find the business development approach that suits you best.

Below is a list of some of the various ways in which you can be successful in business development.

Present at conferences.

One could argue that the difference between an introverted lawyer and an extroverted lawyer is that an introverted lawyer will go to a conference if he is making a presentation, but skip social events like cocktail receptions, while an extroverted lawyer only wants to go to the conference's social events, and skip the presentations. Presenting at conferences was my favorite approach to business development, and I confess I am an introvert.

Presenting at conferences gives you a chance to showcase your wares and your personality from a position of purpose. I didn't realize it the first time I spoke at a conference, but simply being a speaker at a conference gives you an aura of expertise. The audience simply assumes, without question, that you are an expert or you wouldn't be giving the presentation. When you discuss a topic to a room full of people who are interested in the topic (or they wouldn't be there), and when an entire room full of people see you as an expert and see a sample of your personality, developing business from that point is relatively easy. Most often when I finished a presentation, a small group of people would approach me to ask follow-up questions and dive deeper into the topic. It's kind of the same point where you want to find yourself in a traditional networking event, but without the painfully awkward small talk and without needing to suss out who in the room is at all interested in your area of expertise.

It is very important to understand that speaking at a conference is the beginning of the business development process. After speaking at a conference, I would exchange contact information with those who showed interest. I would receive follow-up phone calls and emails, and most important of all, I would send follow-up emails and make follow-up phone calls.

Write articles.

Writing on areas within your subject matter expertise for the many print and online legal journals is an excellent way to develop business, because it builds your credibility and reaches a vast audience. In a way, this is like presenting at conferences, but the results are in slow motion. Just as with presenting at a conference, when you write an article you are showcasing your expertise and you are also able to show a little of your personality to your audience. And just as with presenting at a conference, you are speaking to an audience who is already interested in the topic (or they wouldn't read the article). There are differences, of course. One difference is that it does not enable you to interact with your audience at your initiative, but only at their initiative; only if they reach out to you after having read your article. Another difference is the timeline.

The time it takes to write an article is about the same as the time it takes to prepare a high-quality presentation for a conference, but the time it takes to receive any feedback is different.

There is a delay between the day you finish the article and the day it is published. There is another delay between the day it is published and the day people begin to read it. And then of course there is another delay between the day anyone reads the article and the day they reach out to you.

There is, however, a very effective use of a published article that can accelerate the follow-up stage of the process and enable you to take an active role, rather than passive. The day the article is published you send it to all of your contacts with a nice cover note. The note can say anything, even something as simple as: "I thought you might like to see this article I wrote on XYZ." Having published an article will give you tremendous credibility on its topic, and nearly all of your contacts to whom you send the article will reply to you, even if only to say thank you.

Meet Clients one-on-one.

Meeting potential Clients for coffee, lunch or consultation one-on-one is very powerful, because you have their full attention and because there are no distractions. Because there are no other people vying for the attention of the potential Client, and because there is no audience of third parties listening in on the conversation, it is easy to focus on the topic at hand when meeting one-on-one. Meeting potential Clients in person, one-on-one, was one of my favorite methods of business development. Of course, I was presenting at conferences two or three times each quarter and so I maintained a pipeline of potential Clients for one-on-one meetings. And that is the trick. If meeting one-on-one is going to work as a business development approach, you must create a meaningful pipeline of people with whom to have such one-on-one meetings. Fortunately, any and all of the other business development approaches discussed in this Chapter will enable you to create such a pipeline.

Praise others often.

Speak highly of others when they are not in your presence. This is related to the discussion in Chapter 35 *Give as much credit to others as possible*, in which I described the Credit/Credibility Paradox (i.e., giving others credit increases your own credibility). When you speak highly of others in their absence it has several positive ramifications, each of which increases your credibility and thus your ability to attract business. First, your audience is receiving a subconscious message that you probably speak highly of them in their absences. Second, it will very likely get back to the person of whom you spoke highly that you were praising them and they will very much like you for it. Third, it has the benefit of truth. In fact, I should caution that this technique is only appropriate when truthful. The good news is that nearly everyone is deserving of praise in some respect. If a person is a misanthrope but also a genius you can speak highly of their intellectual prowess. If a person is affable but also a dimwit, you can speak highly of their charm. To be clear, praising others in their absence is a form of business development. It is a crucial aspect of establishing your character in a network of lawyers and potential Clients. It shows others what they can expect of you if they choose to work with you. It also attracts others to you, because the key to someone liking you is for them to know that you like them. Potential Clients who know you like them, who hear you have spoken highly of them, will seek you out. This is even more true of colleagues in your law firm, and colleagues in your law firm are a tremendous source of business, discussed below.

Focus on your colleagues.

Business development is not limited to mining relationships with strangers. For me, mining relationships with total strangers was unpleasant, terrifying and unfruitful. But at some point, early my career I realized that nearly every kind of Client I could ever want was already a Client of my firm in some capacity. Better yet, I realized I had an extraordinary network already established rendering moot the need to go build a network from scratch. Sure, the people in my network may not have thought of themselves as being my network, but that didn't matter. My network comprised my colleagues throughout my law firm. It was a pleasant moment when I realized I had a network already built, rendering unnecessary the painful process of networking from scratch. I had tremendous success mining my network of colleagues for opportunities. Developing business within your own law firm still requires effort, however, because (i) you must take affirmative steps to ensure your colleagues know who you are and what skills you have and (ii) you must build a reputation as an excellent and likeable lawyer, which you can accomplish by implementing the elements of this book in your practice.

Do extraordinarily good work.

In the early years of your career, you are likely to be told what work to do. Business development will seem like a concern for some distant future. But the truth is you are developing business from the moment you receive your first assignment. Some lawyers build a successful career by doing nothing—literally nothing—beyond doing extraordinarily good work. They receive an assignment from a Partner and do an excellent job. Word gets around.

They get more work, and they continue to do excellent work. Eventually, Clients begin to reach out to them directly and assign them tasks. They continue to do an excellent job. So far, none of this has resulted in any new Clients, but it will have expanded the amount of work coming from existing Clients. Expanding the amount of work from existing Clients is a solid baseline level of successful business development. The higher level of business development success is achieved when you land a new Client who has not worked with your law firm before at all. It is possible to reach even the higher level of business development success doing nothing more than extraordinarily good work. This is because at some point a Client or a colleague will refer a potential Client to you solely on the basis of the excellent work you have done. At such moment you will either need to meet with the potential Client, engaging in some form of business development beyond just doing legal work, or on rare occasion the strength of the referral may itself lead to an initial assignment from the new Client. If you do extraordinarily good work on such initial assignment, then voila, you have a new Client and have achieved the higher level of business development success. Keep in mind that your colleagues will only introduce you to potential Clients if both (i) and (ii) under "Focus on your colleagues" above are true.

Attend large networking events.

Large-format networking events range from Bar Association gatherings to firm-sponsored cocktail parties, charity events and so on. The purpose of these events is to create a venue for meeting others that you might be able to work with or work for, as the case may be. These events often involve large numbers of people, most of whom do not know most of the other people in attendance. Because the events are designed for networking, and are not merely gatherings at random, they are a fraction better than trying to develop business in an airport, shopping mall, train terminal or other crowded place full of strangers. (Unfortunately for the rest of us, there are lawyers who will in fact try to develop business in every location I just mentioned. Uhg.)

One friend of mine who is a successful Partner at a prestigious law firm considers large networking events to be most valuable if you become involved in the planning of such events. Involving yourself in the planning of such events creates more meaningful contacts with others involved, and gives you a credibility boost before even entering the room on the day of the event. But even those who are not involved in planning an event might thrive in a large-format environment. There were certainly a number of people at my law firm who were constantly going to networking events and chasing down the leads they obtained at such events. So, like each of the approaches discussed in this Chapter and even those not covered in this Chapter, the approach will be effective if it suits your personality.

Combine multiple approaches.

In reality, successful lawyers use a combination of the various approaches to business development described above. My advice is not to spend a lot of time focused on something you do not like doing and, as a result, are not good at doing. Rather, find the business development approaches that you enjoy and focus on those approaches. I am certain that, at a minimum, you will be more successful using approaches you enjoy than approaches you do not enjoy.

One thing to note about all of the approaches to business development is that they take a substantial commitment of time, often building slowly over many years. It is never too early to start, but it can be too early to expect unrealistic results. You are extremely unlikely to land a major corporate Client in your first few years of practicing law, for example. If an executive at a major corporation has an important legal issue that needs to be handled, they are almost certain to hire a lawyer with many years of experience. Alas, to be the lawyer who gets hired once you have many years of experience, you will need to have been business developing all along the way, using one or more of the approaches described above.

31

Are Partners bad managers?

There is a bizarre refrain out in the legal industry which states, "Partners in law firms are bad managers." Meanwhile, law firm Partners continue to make extraordinary sums of money. In fact, other than recessions, Partners in law firms have made more money every year consecutively since data started to be gathered on law firms. Clearly, Partners at law firms are managing their law practices well.

Because the myth "Partners are bad managers" is ubiquitous, it is worth our time to probe a little by asking the question, "What are they so bad at managing?" But in order to answer that question, we must first ask, "What do Partners manage?"

Partners manage the complex interplay among Clients, adverse parties, opposing lawyers, external institutions such as courts and regulators (e.g., SEC, CFTC, FCC, FDIC, DOL, IRS, etc.) and law firm concerns (e.g., navigating conflicts of interests, staffing new matters, reviewing invoices, training Associates and much more), all in the pursuit of increased profits for the Partners. Viewed from this perspective, all must agree that law firm Partners are excellent managers. Partner profits in law firms rise steadily, year after year after year (excluding recessions).

It is clear that Partners at law firms are excellent managers in respect of those areas they are managing that impact the success of their law firms. So, what is it that they are so bad at managing?

The answer: Partners are bad at managing Associates. In other words, the statement, "Partners are bad managers" really means,

"Partners are bad managers of Associates." Importantly, the criticism is from the perspective of Associates and not from the perspective of Clients, the firms' equity owners, or any governing body related to the firms. Clients are happy with how Partners manage cases and transactions or they would hire other lawyers. The firms' equity owners are happy with the profits being created by the Partners or they would change the manner in which Partners pursue profits. Ditto for advisory boards, executive committees and so on—if they were not happy, they would make changes to the firms' approaches. But the criticism is valid from the perspective of Associates and worthy of your attention, because the shortcomings of Partners at law firms vis-à-vis you as an Associate can have tremendous impacts on your career.

Perhaps the most significant way in which Partners are bad managers of Associates is that Partners have a tendency to avoid unpleasant confrontation within the halls of their own law firms. It is really quite interesting that some of the most skilled human beings on the planet at impactful confrontation, those who routinely go into verbal battle on behalf of Clients, are not able to stomach unpleasant conversations with their own employees. Two factors lead to this counter-intuitive reality. First, because Partners expend so much of their energy engaged in verbal confrontations on behalf of Clients, they have little appetite for it thereafter. Second, Partners consider their law firm a fortress from which they wage their intellectual wars in the practice of law; all those within the fortress walls are bound by an unwritten pact of mutual protection and support.

In light of the two factors I set forth above, imagine the difficulty a Partner has in confronting an underperforming Associate. It is enough of a challenge to find ways to provide helpful feedback on projects, but the really tough conversations—the conversations about an Associate's future (or lack thereof) at the law firm—those often get pushed off until a later date that never comes. Partners often cannot muster the grit to approach an Associate with truly bad career news. Partners do not have the emotional energy, because they spend it all on battles for Clients; they also find it uncomfortable to violate the unwritten pact of solidarity I mentioned above.

What this means for you as a Junior Associate is that you must be assertive (though never rude) and insist on a clear understanding from Partners of your status and prospects at the firm. The more precise your questions, the better able Partners will be to give you candid insights. Do not assume that Partners can anticipate what you need to know, and definitely do not assume that they will tell you unsolicited what you need to know. Think carefully about what you need to know and then persistently pursue Partners until you get what you need. Caveat: Once you have the information you need, do not pester Partners simply because you enjoy hearing that you are doing a good job.

There is another tip I want to give you in light of the ubiquitous phrase that Partners are bad managers. You will not build goodwill with Partners by repeating it. I tended to resent those who made the statement, and the less experience the speaker had who made the statement, the more I resented him. My resentment was tied to my many years of hard work as a Partner and manager in a law firm. I assure you that many Partners feel the same way I did. The phrase is stated frequently enough in the profession of law that you might mistakenly think it is a universally held belief and, more, that such belief is unoffensive. Note that the phrase is not universally believed and is considered by many Partners to be offensive. I recommend that you refrain from making the statement, or at least exercise enough good judgment to not make the statement in front of Partners.

32

Every Client is the most important Client.

It is important to convey to each Client that such Client is your most important Client. Before focusing on Clients, however, I want to discuss your superiors, your peers and your subordinates.

Superiors

For most of you reading this book, your work superiors will be Partners at your law firm, as well as other Associates who have more seniority than you. To a Junior Associate, all Partners are important and some Senior Associates seem for all practical purposes as important as Partners.

I recall working on an initial public offering (IPO) of a company's common stock in 1999. I was a Junior Associate. I was part of a team that included me, a Mid-Level Associate, a Senior Associate, a Junior Partner and a Senior Partner. At the time, I was also working on a merger of two private companies. The merger project was similarly staffed with me, a Mid-Level Associate, a Senior Associate, a Junior Partner and a Senior Partner. To me at that time there was no distinction between the four Partners I mention above, nor was there any distinction between the four

Associates that had seniority over me. In my mind, they all had authority over me and as such were equally important.

One day, I received requests on both projects. Both needed tasks done immediately, and either task would take me the full day to complete. Clearly, I could not do both in the same day. I would be able to do one on the day of the request and the other would have to wait until the next day. Now, if I had some preconception of the relative importance of the various Partners and Associates on the two matters, I may have tried to make some calculation as to which team was more important and do the work of the more important team. But understanding the equality of each project and each team, equal in my eyes and from my perspective, saved me from such a blunder. I viewed both teams as equally important. So, I replied to both teams and explained that the two requests had come to me simultaneously and that I needed their help to prioritize. I noted to the Partners on both teams that, to me, this seemed to be a clash of the titans and I had little hope of surviving in such a contest. I was happy to do first whichever project they, the titans, decided among themselves I should do first. Within an hour, I received a reply as to which I should do first and there was no incident.

A friend of mine found himself in a very similar situation, but made the mistake of prioritizing one project ahead of another on the basis of which team he perceived as being more important. He proceeded accordingly without notifying either team. It was an unpleasant experience for him, to say the least. In that one decision, he had offended four superiors (i.e., the two Partners and two Associates that were on the team he de-prioritized) and, to boot, he misjudged which project to prioritize. As it turned out, the two projects were not equally time sensitive. Just because both teams had made an urgent request, did not mean that the tasks were in fact equally urgent. The project he ignored related to a bank regulatory filing that needed to be made by close of East Coast banking hours the following day, which was 2 p.m. Pacific. The project itself would take my friend all day to complete and that would leave only the following morning and early afternoon to make any corrections and finalize the filing. The other project involved revising a draft contract and was not subject to a regulatory filing deadline. When the bank-filing team learned the next morning that he had prioritized the contract-assignment team and had not even started on the bank filing project, a pall of dismay descended on the office which gave way to frenetic desperation as the more experienced lawyers jumped to the task of preparing the filing themselves in the remaining time.

My advice, therefore, is to operate under the belief that your superiors and their matters are all equal even if in your heart of hearts you think you know who is more important than whom, and even if you think you know which tasks are more important than others. Remember that you have not earned the right to make judgments as to who is more important than whom nor to decide which tasks are more important than others. In addition to it being arrogant for you, as a Junior Associate, to believe you know such things, it is an unnecessary risk to make such a decision for yourself. It is foolish to take on such an unnecessary risk so early in your career. During the early years of your career, it is appropriate—critical, really—to reach out to your superiors and ask them which tasks to prioritize.

Peers

With respect to your peers, treating them all equality is important to building a supportive network. Perhaps not all of your peers will be your friends, but many might be if you treat them all equally.

Why would anyone not treat peers as equals, given that is the essence of a "peer," is it not? And why do you need friends at work?

Why would anyone not treat peers as equals?

Because the practice of law tends to attract highly competitive personalities and because it also attracts individuals who have advanced in life on the basis of their intelligence being superior relative to others, it is an unfortunate fact that many Junior Associates arrive at a law firm obsessed with determining how they measure up to the other Junior Associates and how the other Junior Associates measure up among each other. I would recommend against engaging in this misguided exercise altogether, but I am not sure it is possible to ask Junior Associates whose entire lives have been driven by being graded and ranked to suddenly stop comparing themselves to their peers. As such, my advice is to resist the temptation to allow your assessments of the relative abilities of your peers to dictate how you will interact with your peers. Why? Because you are likely to be wrong in your assessments!

Take, as an example, my experience in law school. Early in the first year of law school my peers began forming study groups. It was not until my second year of law school that I learned of these study groups. It turned out that I had not been invited to join anyone's study group. I was not perceived as being smart. I had not attended an Ivy League college and was never pretentious with my knowledge. I had conveyed nothing to others to suggest I was smart, and so they skipped me in their attempts to construct study groups of only the smart students. I was always more interested in finding the fun in life, and many people erroneous think that fun-seeking is incompatible with intelligence. In my lifetime, the reverse has been true. Silliness is the outward expression of brilliance, because what others struggle in great seriousness to discern, a brilliant man finds comically easy.

It was also the case that the students in these groups tended to keep the groups somewhat secret, or perhaps I was never the gossipy type and so I was outside the loop of informal information. Slowly, during my second year of law school I learned of the various study groups. One of these study groups gained a reputation of being the most secretive and having the best students. They were nicknamed by the rest of the student body as the Double Secret Study Group poking a little fun at them by alluding to the movie Animal House and the absurd concept of "Double Secret Probation." Well, I assumed like everybody else that the students in the Double Secret Study Group were the best students. They certainly seemed smart to me. They were well-prepared for classes. They spoke confidently when called on by professors, and even when not called upon by professors.

Not having been invited to join any study group freed me to be on friendly terms with students across all the existing study groups. I treated all my fellow students equally. It freed me to ask any of them for help from time to time when a new legal concept was not making sense to me. I didn't study with any of them, but I was free to ask any of them a question here and there. I had unintentionally developed a very broad-based network of friends who could help me, albeit on an ad hoc basis. But ad hoc was perfect for me, as there was not any pattern as to which concepts I would grasp quickly versus those that I found challenging. I think if I had been in a study group, most of my time would have been wasted on concepts I had no problem understanding on my own.

It was not until riding in a car during the summer after graduating from law school that I learned the truth about study groups and the fallacy of assessing one's peers. A significant majority of students from my law school stayed for the summer in Charlottesville, VA after graduation to study for the Bar Exam. During this summer, personalities relaxed a little, study groups dissolved into obsoletion, and there was greater mingling among the former cliques. I found myself in a car riding with four of the students from the disbanded Double Secret Study Group; these were classmates with whom I had not spent much time during the prior three years of law school. I sat quietly, enjoying the opportunity to hear the smartest among our class carry on their conversation. One of them began to complain about the strict bell curve, or "B mean," that was required at my law school. This meant that professors were obligated to grade exams on a double-blind system and allocate grades in a manner that resulted in a mean grade of B (subsequently increased to B+ in 1997) for the class as a whole. The B mean irked him, because he had a sibling studying for a Master of Arts in History and in the History Program it was unusual for a graduate student not to receive mostly A grades; there was no required bell curve for the outcomes in the History Program.

Then it happened, as we were riding along in the car, a moment that remains as a flashbulb memory for me. One of the former members of the Double Secret Study Group said, commiserating with the first, "Hey, that B mean kept me from getting a single A." Then the other said, "Well, I only had one A." A third said, "we didn't get many As, but we all got good jobs, so who cares?"

I was kind of dizzy, like I wasn't really hearing what I was hearing. These were four of the smartest students in our class, supposedly, and none had received more than a single A in all of law school! I had received a good number of A grades throughout law school. I knew we had a B mean, and I had plenty of Bs to be sure, but I figured these guys from the Double Secret Study Group must be getting more A grades than me. After all, I wasn't in any study group at all.

The same human nature that leads to cliques in law school tempts the less-mature lawyers at a law firm to try and silently rank all Junior Associates. But just as in law school, I did not gravitate toward any particular clique at my law firm and instead treated all of my peers equally. Just as in law school, being clique-free at my law firm gave me a broad base of friends across the law firm. Of course, I had my opinions about the abilities of each of my peers, but I simply saw no point in grouping off into cliques. And truthfully, trying to differentiate the intelligence of the Junior Associates at my law firm was futile—they were all very smart or they wouldn't have been there!

Why does one need friends in a law firm?

Sometimes the most basic questions are the hardest to answer. The question, "Why does one need friends in a law firm?" is such a question. I suspect every person who has ever worked at a law firm would have a dozen answers to this question and each of their answers would differ to some degree from the answers given by each other person. There is little use in trying to enumerate all of the reasons it is important to have friends at a law firm, but there are two very important reasons worth noting.

First, without friends at a law firm you have no one to turn to with questions. Without friends, you will be on your own to solve every challenge. Sure, you might have been assigned a mentor and perhaps you feel comfortable approaching Partners with your questions, but the truth is that mentors and Partners do not have much free time to answer all the little questions that come up during your first few years practicing law. Having friends at the law firm will give you a network to tap with your questions. If 10 of you know 10% of all that you need to know to survive and succeed, there is chance that together as friends you know 100% of all you need to know.

Second, the early years of practicing law are isolating and harsh. You do not have much time to spend with friends outside of the law firm. If you have no friends in the law firm, you will find yourself lonely and discontent. Having friends in a law firm is very important from an emotional wellbeing perspective to your ability to survive and succeed at the law firm.

Subordinates

With respect to subordinates, such as secretaries, paralegals, librarians, Human Resources and so on, the critical point I want to make is that you are much better served viewing them as peers, rather than subordinates. Viewed as peers, you need only read the section above to understand how to survive and succeed. The same benefits that result from treating all peers as equals will result from treating all subordinates as equals—i.e., having a robust network of advisers and friends to help in myriad challenges during your career. Plus, one never knows the future—a subordinate today could be a Client tomorrow.

Clients

I saved the best for last. In many ways, the benefits of avoiding preferential treatment of some Clients over others are a combination of the benefits described above under *Superiors, Peers* and *Subordinates.* Just as with your superiors in the law firm, it is important not to have one Client think you have chosen to provide service to another Client ahead of them or with more enthusiasm. And just as it with your peers and subordinates in the law firm, it is important to develop a network among your Clients, ideally as friends. But unlike your superiors, peers and subordinates, to whom you convey the message that all are equally important, for Clients you must convey that every Client is your most important Client.

How can this be, you ask? How can every Client be my most important Client? Some Clients pay higher rates than other Clients. Some Clients provide significantly more work than other Clients. And some Clients are much easier to interact with than other Clients, by being less insulting, less demanding or even genuinely nice people. Considering that, on the one hand, some Clients pay high rates, provide a heavy flow of work and are genuinely nice people while, on the other hand, some Clients whittle you down on rates, have only sporadic need for legal services and are rude in their interactions, it is abundantly clear that some Clients are more important to you than other Clients. But, to survive in a law firm and ultimately to be successful you must develop the ability to convey to each Client that such Client is your most important Client.

My approach was to remind myself of the simple truth that when focused on a Client, that Client is my most important Client. When I am on a call with a Client, in negotiations on behalf of a Client, conducting legal research for a Client, drafting a contract for a Client, and so on, it is that Client who is my most important Client. And ethically, is this not the way it should be? Surely, every Client deserves your best efforts and zealous representation while you are focused on their matters. Surely, as you are doing work for and with a Client, such Client is your most important Client.

A great example of the importance of understanding that every Client is your most important Client is *pro bono*. When I was a Junior Associate, I made a mistake that I saw other Junior Associates repeat time and time again throughout my career. I relegated my *pro bono* Clients to the bottom of my to-do list. It was not until a wise and honest Partner stared me in the eyes and asked me to explain why a *pro bono* Client was any less of a Client under the law than a Client paying full rates? I was embarrassed, in fact I was ashamed, to admit that the only reason I had treated the *pro bono* Client as a second-class Client was the fact that a *pro bono* Client was not paying for our legal services. The Partner pointed out the obvious, which is that *pro bono* Clients do not pay for legal services because they cannot pay for legal services. Their need of legal representation is no less valid. Fearing that I might be a soulless money-grubber, the Partner then added that regardless of my value system when it comes to who can and who cannot pay for legal services, the fact is that a *pro bono* Client is a Client that (i) can sue for malpractice and (ii) is owed all of the same fiduciary obligations from us as lawyers as any other Client, including without limitation, the duty of zealous representation, the duty of candor, all of the Ethics Rules and so on. From then on, I treated every Client as my most important Client as and when I handled their legal matters.

33

MANAGE YOUR CALENDAR OR DROWN IN A SEA OF DEMANDS.

You will learn at some point early in your career, if you have not already, that the traditional business hours of a day tend to be consumed by activities involving interaction with others and the evenings and weekends are therefore the only time you can do the work that must be done by you, alone, before the traditional business hours resume.

A typical week goes something like this …

> On **Monday** afternoon, you are assigned to a new case, and it is now the fifth different project you have on your plate at the time. The Partner leading the case asks you to conduct research and draft a memorandum on certain questions of law. The Partner has never worked with you before, but has heard good things—your reputation is off to a good start at the law firm. The memorandum is due by open of business on Friday morning. You are eager to work on the new case; it sounds interesting and having an entire week to research a finite area of law and write a memorandum sounds pretty easy to you.
>
> You do not turn to the new assignment on Monday evening, because you are finishing up a different assign-

ment. You decide you will start on the new assignment on Tuesday.

On **Tuesday**, the Partner leading the new case calls together you and the rest of the team to discuss strategy for the case and brainstorm. You also must participate in two other conference calls that were scheduled days earlier, and of course you must prepare for each. Meanwhile, during the course of Tuesday you receive dozens of emails from various Senior Associates and Partners, most of which are titled something like "Quick Question" or "Quick Favor" and require you to stop whatever you are doing to chase down an answer, before turning back to your existing assignments. You begin to feel hungry and realize that it is already 7 p.m. You are still tackling the "Quick Question" emails, so you decide to finish those and then grab dinner. At 8 p.m., you can finally turn to the research assignment on the new case. By 10 p.m. you realize the assignment is far more complicated than you originally thought. All of sudden the Friday morning deadline seems far more challenging than when you received the assignment, but you calm yourself down by reminding yourself that you still have Wednesday and Thursday to get it done. By midnight on Tuesday, you are feeling tired and, knowing you have days left to get the assignment done, you go home.

Wednesday morning you awake to several emails requesting that you participate on conference calls for three of your ongoing projects and another strategy meeting is being scheduled for the new case. After confirming you will join each, you see that your calendar for Wednesday is booked almost back-to-back from 9 a.m. until

7 p.m. During the course of Wednesday, more "Quick Question" and "Quick Favor" emails arrive, and you start to feel as if requests are rising all around you like flood waters growing steadily. A short bolt of panic pulses in your veins. You think about the research project you have for the new case, which is due on Friday morning. You still have Wednesday evening and all of Thursday to get it done. But the "Quick Question" and "Quick Favor" emails have stacked up during your conference calls and meetings on Wednesday and it will take you until midnight to respond to all of those before you can think about turning to the new research assignment. Finally, you are able to turn your attention to the new assignment at midnight. You are tired, but you know you must get something done on the assignment if you have any hope of meeting the Friday morning deadline. You work until 2 a.m. and are simply too tired to push further.

On **Thursday** morning, another slew of emails has arrived before you awake. You look at your calendar and again you have several conference calls and meetings lined up. Some of the emails are seeking to add conference calls to the day, and there are some open times on your calendar; so, you reply confirming that you will join those—what choice do you have? Another day quickly disappears in a flurry of conference calls and "Quick Question" and "Quick Favor" emails. Before you know it, hunger rises in you and you see that it is past 7 p.m. You grab a quick dinner and turn back to work. Now it is 8 p.m. on Thursday evening. You are down to your last evening to get the research assignment done on your new case. You clear out the lingering "Quick Question" and

"Quick Favor" emails and at 10 p.m. you start again on the new assignment. A calm feeling comes over you as you accept that you will need to work all night to complete the assignment on time. You grab a cup of coffee and begin working. At midnight you feel a little tired, so you grab another cup of coffee. At 2 a.m. you are really tired, so you grab another cup of coffee. By 4 a.m., you feel an odd surge of adrenaline, surprisingly it is kind of fun to work through the silent hours of the night—you are at peace, no new emails have arrived in hours and you are making great progress on your assignment. You think to yourself, and find it humorous, that you enjoy your job most between midnight and morning. Your research is complete and all you have to do is write the memorandum. You begin cobbling together a draft of the memorandum. 7 a.m. comes quickly and the memorandum is complete, but you know it is not refined at all. It reads as if someone tried to use sentences to create a Jackson Pollok painting; concepts are splattered all over the place and cases have been dumped in at random. The good news is that you feel strong that all of the case law is captured. The bad news is that you know if you had more time, you could create a really good memorandum.

At 8 a.m. **Friday** morning the Partner who gave you the assignment asks if you can bring a draft of your memorandum to her office at 10 a.m. You feel a tiny moment of relief. You have two hours to clean up the memorandum. You have not yet slept, but you are still riding the adrenaline and caffeine high from the wee hours of last night. At 9:55 a.m., you know it will take you 5 minutes to catch the elevator to the Partner's floor and so you print your draft memorandum, grab it and head to the Partner's office. You think to yourself what an amazing amount of work you were able to accomplish in one all-nighter. The cleanup you did on the memorandum went smoothly, and you feel that it is pretty damn good given the tight timing.

You walk into the Partner's office and she looks well rested, wearing a nice outfit and sitting behind a large desk in her large Partner's office. She notices you seem a little disheveled, but she doesn't know you well—maybe this is how you always look? She says good morning to you and notes what a beautiful Friday it is outside. You hadn't noticed, nor have you been outside in more than 24 hours since arriving at work on Thursday morning, but you manage to reply saying something vague and polite. Now you sit and wait, silently, while the Partner reads your draft memorandum. Your stomach does a little flip as the Partner begins to write something on your draft in sharp jerking movements of a pen, then you see her cross out whole sections of your memorandum. It is like you handed over your first born and this monster is taking a dagger and carving it up. The pen motions get more severe. The Partner glances up at you with a frown, then back down to the draft. More scribbling and crossing out of things and now she is sighing, and shifting her weight in her chair. At least half an hour passes while you sit silently watching and wondering, is it as bad as it seems? Finally, she speaks while handing the draft memorandum back to you. "Well, the good news is I am giving you until Monday morning to try again." You feel a rush of anger and disappointment. You just worked all night and the Partner either doesn't know or doesn't care. You know the work isn't perfect, but that's because you ran out of time, which is because this mean Partner didn't give you enough time. Your anger surprises you, and you're not sure why but perhaps it is because you always received good grades and praise in life and now someone has taken an assignment from you and torn it apart in half an hour. Even more unsettling is that the Partner had nothing to say other than do it over. No praise. No thanks.

Somewhere in your heart of hearts you know that this Partner is now concerned that you do not have what it takes to be a successful lawyer in the law firm. Your first impression—the very first work product this Partner has ever seen from you—was a sloppy, chaotic memorandum.

Your reward for working all night is to work all weekend and deliver a much-improved memorandum by Monday morning.

The week described above could have gone very differently with a few skills on how to manage a calendar, and more specifically how to use the calendar as a tool to protect you against dismal outcomes.

The week described above is the kind of week I experienced as a Junior Associate. But let me show you how the week would have gone using the calendar skills I developed later in my career. I hope you are able to use these early in your career.

On **Monday** afternoon, you are assigned to a new case, and it is now the fifth different project you have on your plate at the time. The Partner leading the case asks you to conduct research and draft a memorandum on certain questions of law. The Partner has never worked with you before, but has heard good things—your reputation is off to a good start at the law firm. The memorandum is due by open of business on Friday morning. You are eager to work on the new case; it sounds interesting and having an entire week to research a finite area of law and write a memorandum sounds pretty easy to you.

You open your calendar and see that you had blocked off a three-hour time period on Tuesday afternoon and a four-hour time period on Wednesday afternoon. These appointments say only "Office Hours," which is your code for a time that you have reserved to get tasks done during the day. You learned that reserving three-hour and four-hour blocks of time, two or three days each week, helps reduce the number of late nights you spend in the office as and when new assignments come your way—and new assignments always come your way. You immediately update the calendar and rename those blocks of time "New Case Project." Now, you have preserved 7 hours of time to work on the assignment before you have even started.

On **Tuesday**, the Partner leading the new case calls together you and the rest of the team to discuss strategy for the case and brainstorm. But this is not too challenging, because you had only one other conference call scheduled for Tuesday and the already blocked-off time (now dedicated for the new project). During the course of Tuesday, you receive dozens of emails from various Senior Associates and Partners, most of which are titled something like "Quick Question" or "Quick Favor." These request that you stop whatever you are doing to chase down an answer, before resuming to your existing assignments. Thankfully, because your calendar shows others that you are in a meeting, some of those requests are rerouted to other Junior Associates or can wait. Rather than disrupt your flow of thought, you will reply to all such emails at the end of the blocked off time. You spend three hours Tuesday afternoon doing research for the new assignment. At 5 p.m. you begin to tackle the "Quick Question" and "Quick Favor" emails. Many were already addressed by others, so you provide answers on the remaining. You begin to feel hungry and realize that it is already 7 p.m. At 8 p.m., after your dinner, you turn back to the research assignment on the new case. By 10 p.m. you have completed a total of five hours on the assignment and it's only Tuesday evening. You decide that the complexity of the assignment warrants some extra efforts and you stay until midnight. When you leave the office on Tuesday you feel good that you have already made seven hours of progress on the new assignment.

Wednesday morning you awake to several emails requesting that you participate on conference calls on three of your ongoing projects and another strategy meeting is being scheduled for the new case. Because you had already blocked off a four-hour chunk of time on your calendar, which you retitled as New Research Project, you cannot accept all of the requests for conference calls. Instead, you look ahead to your schedule on Thursday and Friday and reply with proposals for different times. To this you receive different types of replies, some saying "No problem, the new time you proposed works" and some saying "It is not critical that you be on the call, we can fill you in later." During the course of Wednesday, more "Quick Question" and "Quick Favor" emails arrive, and you go through these at two specific times of day—at 1 p.m. and 5 p.m., before and after your dedicated block of time for the new research assignment. Just as on Tuesday, some of the emails are already resolved by the time you check and so you handle those that are not resolved. The batch that came into your inbox between 1 p.m. and 5 p.m. is significant. You will need to spend several hours addressing those, but you are able to turn your attention again to the new research assignment at 9 p.m. You are tired, but you know that working until midnight will allow you to complete all of the research you need before you start writing the memorandum. When you leave at the end of Wednesday, at midnight, you realize you have spent another 7 hours on the new research and memorandum project, which brings the total to 14 hours, and you will have all of Thursday to put together the memorandum from your research.

On **Thursday** morning, another slew of emails has arrived before you awake. You look at your calendar and you have several conference calls and meetings lined up. Some of the emails are seeking to add conference calls to the day, and there are some open times on your calendar; but you reply indicating that your day is booked and note that Friday is clear on your calendar—what choice do you have? You need at least 5 hours to write a good memorandum from your research. You get a variety of responses saying either rescheduling for Friday is fine or that you needn't join the call, after all. Another day quickly disappears with your previously scheduled conference calls and a flurry of "Quick Question" and "Quick Favor" emails, but you still managed to spend a couple of hours on the New Case Memorandum. Before you know it, hunger rises in you and you see that it is past 7 p.m. You grab a quick dinner and turn back to work. Now it is 8 p.m.

on Thursday evening. You are down to your last evening to get the New Case Memorandum completed. By midnight, you have completed the memorandum to your satisfaction—it is as good as you can get it. You decide you will go home and sleep, then review it one last time in the morning before handing it over to the Partner.

At 8 a.m. **Friday** morning the Partner who gave you the assignment asks if you can bring a draft of your memorandum to her office at 10 a.m. No problem, you think to yourself, and you proof the memorandum and make a few further cleanup changes. At 9:55 a.m., you know it will take you 5 minutes to catch the elevator to the Partner's floor and so you print your draft memorandum, grab it and head to the Partners office. You think to yourself, what a pretty Friday it is.

You walk into the Partner's office and she looks well rested, wearing a nice outfit and sitting behind a large desk in her large Partner's office. She says good morning to you and notes what a beautiful Friday it is outside. You reply that you agree. She notices that you look well-rested and dressed nicely. Already you are making a good impression. Now you sit and wait, silently, while the Partner reads your draft memorandum. Your stomach does a little flip as the Partner begins to write something on your draft in sharp jerking movements of a pen, then you see her cross out whole sections of your memorandum. It is like you handed over your first born and this monster is taking a dagger and carving it up. The pen motions get more severe. The Partner glances up at you with a frown, then back down to the draft. More scribbling and crossing out of things and now she is sighing,

> and shifting her weight in her chair. At least half an hour passes while you sit silently watching and wondering, is it as bad as it seems? Finally, she speaks while handing the draft memorandum back to you. "It looks pretty good for a first draft," she says, "but there is a lot that needs to be addressed. I've made my comments and if you have any questions as you work on the rewrite, my door is always open. I need to update the Client on Wednesday, but you have made good progress so I am not too worried. Please have the revised draft back to me by Tuesday morning. It's clear you worked hard on this first draft; thank you."
>
> You leave the office feeling pretty good, she said a few nice things. It's the real world and praise is never effusive like back in school, but somewhere in your heart of hearts you know that this Partner knows you have what it takes to be a successful lawyer in the law firm. Your first impression—the very first work product this Partner has ever seen from you—was a well-researched and well-organized memorandum.
>
> Your reward is that the rewrite will not be difficult and you have until Tuesday to turn it back to the Partner. This project will not require you to work over the weekend.

Just in case it wasn't obvious, let me recap the specific skills that made such an enormous difference in the quality of life of, and the quality of work product generated by, the Associate in the example above. All of the skills relate, directly or indirectly, to using your calendar as a tool for your survival and success.

1. Block off various chunks of time throughout the week on your calendar, using a title like "Office Hours" or "General Meeting," to create buffers against the inevitable extra work.

You cannot predict when such extra work will flow in, but buffers on your calendar will come in handy.

2. If you receive a request for a conference call or meeting and see that you already have the time blocked off for a conference call, a meeting or for your buffer, then propose alternative times in response to the new request. If you are really in a jam, you should propose a time on the weekend, which makes you look totally dedicated to the Client, and they might not accept your proposal. You get the credit of being available over the weekend without the pain.
3. Set email alerts and other functions to call your attention to emails from critical people, such as Partners leading cases you are on, Partners who lead the practice group you are in, Clients and so on. For all other emails, set specific times in the day to check them and clean them out of your in box. For example, I had sound alerts and red text settings for emails from critical people, to whom I would respond immediately, but then would check all other incoming emails once mid-morning, once in the afternoon, once in the evening and a final time before bed.
4. Emergencies are often solved by others if you wait a little while. You will know those emergencies for which you alone are needed and those which can be solved by somebody other than you. Learn to differentiate between these and you will find significantly less chaos in your day.
5. Give yourself the time you need to produce high quality work. The quality (or lack of quality) of your work will be remembered, but the time pressures to produce such work will not.

34

Never expect a Partner to think for you.

One of the quickest ways to annoy a Partner at your law firm is to rely on that Partner to think for you. If Partners at law firms were sitting around bored, they might enjoy the opportunity to think for you. They might want to demonstrate their prowess as lawyers and want to amaze you with their knowledge and deft analyses. But, rest assured, Partners are not sitting around bored. Partners are challenged by a massive amount of thinking they are being paid to do for Clients. They have no desire to think for you. Quite the opposite; when you are hired by a law firm it is for you to lessen the burden already shouldered by Partners.

Do not confuse the need to ask the Partners questions, which is often appropriate, with seeking to have Partners think for you, which is never appropriate. You must accept responsibility for the portion of the thought spectrum, from basic to advanced, that is within your level of competence. You will often hear Partners tell you to "take ownership" of your assignments, but at times they fail to explain exactly what they mean. This Chapter discusses the heart of what it means to take ownership.

During my tenure as a Partner there was an Associate who worked with me from time to time. His name was Michael. He was extremely smart. He had performed very well at all academic levels and ultimately graduated from a good law school. When

Michael joined my team, he seemed a bit shy and after a few months it was clear that he was also terrified to make a mistake. This was not a bad quality in his first year or second year of practicing law, because I was okay with being asked a lot of questions by Michael. His positive qualities outweighed his severe risk aversion—he was very smart; he had an indefatigable work ethic and he had a pleasant disposition. With Michael, I could give him any amount of work and he would get it done in good cheer.

Intelligence, positive attitude and good cheer were enough to carry Michael to the top of the charts in terms of billable hours and performance ratings for his first few years as an Associate. But by his fourth year as an Associate, Michael's unwillingness to be proactive for fear of making a mistake began to overshadow all of his positive qualities. By the time Michael was a Senior Associate, his career was in jeopardy.

Michael's fear of making mistakes was not *per se* a negative quality. It was not the fear of mistakes that overshadowed Michael's intelligence, strong work ethic and positive disposition. It was Michael's unwillingness to think up and implement solutions that became a serious problem as Michael's career evolved.

Michael had become accustomed to receiving instructions from Partners and then reverting to those Partners as questions arose. He would seek his answers from Partners and then dutifully resume his task. He was operating much like first generation artificial intelligence; he was implementing complex instructions but not thinking of solutions and implementing those solutions on his own. Michael was afraid to be proactive as a result of the fear of making mistakes, but it is important to note that Michael had a choice. The fear of making mistakes presented Michael with challenges, but we all have challenges that we must work around, compensate for or resolve to be able to perform at our best. Michael's real problem was his unwillingness to be proactive and problem solve on his own *notwithstanding* his fear of making mistakes. After all, courage is not facing challenges without fear, but rather courage is facing challenges in spite of fear. There is nothing courageous about doing only what you do not fear.

You might think that I am exaggerating the extent to which Michael had a career-threatening problem. Could a colleague who was intelligent, hardworking and pleasant really be at risk of failure? The answer of course depends on the definition of "failure." In Michael's case, it was clear that he really, very much, wanted to make Partner at my law firm. To him, it would be failure to not become a Partner. And one cannot make Partner at a law firm without both the ability to find solutions for difficult problems and the courage to implement such solutions. As one friend of mine who is a litigation Partner at a prestigious law firm said, "An Associate will not make Partner until she can convince the existing Partners that she is able to be first chair in important cases."

The reason Michael's career began to stagnate in his sixth year as a lawyer was that his usefulness as a colleague diminished. The salary Michael was receiving correlated to the hourly billing rate charged to Clients for Michael's time. The hourly billing rate for Michael as a Senior Associate correlated with advanced lawyering. To be valuable as a Senior Associate, Michael needed to take on tasks that required application of significant problem-solving skills. But, to my dismay, Michael was coming to my office with the same frequency to ask the same types of questions in his sixth year of practicing law as he had done in his first year of practicing law. To be fair, they were not the very same questions, he was smart enough to learn any specific answer to any specific question and never ask the same question twice, but he never answered a new question on his own throughout his first six years as an Associate. With Michael, it was always a matter of showing him exactly which dots needed to be connected and then sending him off to connect the dots.

It is fair to ask a Partner a question you cannot answer, but it is not fair to ask a Partner a question you can answer just because it is easier (from your perspective) to ask the Partner. When you do this, you are asking the Partner to think for you. From the Partner's perspective, you will seem incompetent or immature, or perhaps some combination of both. Over time you will be perceived as simply not worth the time and effort to keep you at the law firm. This sounds harsh, but I mean it literally not figuratively. Even Michael, with his intelligence, work ethic and positive disposition was simply not worth having on my team as a Senior Associate if he was not developing significant problem-solving skills. He was growing less and less valuable to my team as time went by, and ultimately not worth it to have him on the team from a literal cost-benefit perspective.

During his sixth year as an Associate, I made it clear to Michael that he could no longer work on my matters unless he changed his approach, entirely. We agreed to two new rules for our working relationship. He was never allowed to come to my office with a problem without having first developed a proposed solution. And, importantly for his aspirations for promotion to Partner, he promised to implement as many of the solutions he developed as possible without coming to me first. In other words, he was forced to develop a solution before speaking with me, and he was then required to make a judgment call as to whether or not his proposed solution would work. And if he thought it would work, he was obligated to move forward with implementing the solution. All of which he was to do without bothering me. I explained that if he could think up and implement solutions, there was no need to take up my time. (I also explained to him what is written in this book in Chapter 6 *You must understand the relative value of your time to the time of others.*)

Changing Michael's approach to practicing law was not like flicking on a light switch, of course. It was a gradual process. But having the two rules described above in place enabled us to course-correct Michael before it was too late. All in all, I think we together found a good path for Michael. As he developed more and more solutions, he became more and more comfortable doing so. And as he implemented more and more solutions without any input from Partners, he began to exist in a way identifiable as separate and apart from the Partners he worked for; he began to evolve into the kind of Associate that would clearly become a Partner. He is now a thriving Partner.

But did Michael ever get over his fear of making mistakes? No, I do not think so. I believe most of us have some fear of making mistakes and very few of us ever get over that fear. I believe we all develop skills to help us have the courage to move forward in our careers in spite of such fears.

There are lessons for everyone to learn from Michael's story. The lesson for an Associate is, whether or not you are shy, whether or not you are afraid to make mistakes, you can benefit from the two rules Michael began to live by: Never bring a problem to a Partner without a proposed solution; and whenever possible, attempt to implement your solution without involving the Partner. The lesson for me and other Partners is that these two rules should be enforced on Associates early in their careers (perhaps from the first day they arrive); I should not have allowed Michael to attain his sixth year of practice before confronting him on the importance of these two rules.

Even as I type this, I can feel Partners around the world cringing—is Paul McCoy really telling Associates to run wild implementing so-called solutions without Partner oversight and approvals? No, of course not. When I suggest implementing your solutions without involving the Partner who is managing the project, what I am saying is that if you already have instructions from a Partner to accomplish a particular task, and you already have the insights and perspectives you need from the Partner to accomplish such task, there is no reason to go back and use up more of the Partner's time to confirm for your own comfort that your solution is, in fact, consistent with those instructions, insights and perspectives.

Above, I explained how failing to think for yourself limits your usefulness to a law firm. Note that there is another reason it is unwise to ask Partners to think for you. It prevents meaningful bonding and mentoring between you and the Partner.

Your reaction might be, "What? How can it be possible that bringing questions to a Partner would prevent bonding and mentoring? Isn't the primary method of bonding and mentoring between Partner and Associate the question-and-answer process, in some form or another?"

Yes, usually, but sometimes no. Let me explain.

It all comes down to risk sharing versus risk allocating. If you ask questions within a paradigm of a unified team looking to succeed together, willing to shoulder risks together, then yes over time your questions and the subsequent discussions between you and the Partner will create bonds between you and likely create some degree of a mentor-mentee relationship. If, however, you ask questions within a paradigm of division between yourself and the Partner, thinking only what is safest for you and seeking to ensure that all risk lies with the Partner without regard for the success or failure of the team as a whole, then your questions and subsequent discussions between you and the Partner will not create any bonds between you and the Partner, nor will there develop any meaningful mentor-mentee relationship. In the paradigm in which there is division between you and the Partner, no amount of time will lead to any bonding and no amount of questions and discussion will lead to meaningful mentor-mentee relationships. It is likely that the opposite will occur over time, as the Partner consciously or subconsciously begins to think of you as existing adversely to his best interests. How else could he view you if you are always seeking to ensure you have no risk and he has all the risk?

The fact that a Partner carries more responsibility for the success or failure of projects only exacerbates the repellent effect of the paradigm of division. It is already true, regardless of paradigm, that the Partner shoulders the bulk of the responsibility, and is already expected to solve most problems and answer most questions. In either paradigm—unity or division—the Associate will inevitably bring questions to the Partner. What will differ depending on the paradigm is the quantity and nature of the questions brought by an Associate to the Partner. In the paradigm of division, an Associate will bring many (if not all) questions the Partner, because the Associate is seeking to have all risk lie with the Partner. If the Partner is required to answer all questions, the Associate cannot be blamed for any mistakes. In the paradigm of unity, however, an Associate will bring to the Partner only those questions that the Associate is genuinely unable to answer. Thus, in the paradigm of unity, an Associate will bring fewer questions to a Partner and the nature of the questions brought to a Partner will be limited to those beyond the capabilities of the Associate. The Associate will answer all questions within the Associate's capabilities, because the Associate in the paradigm of unity does not view risks as allocated between the Partner and the Associate. Rather, the Associate sees risks as shouldered by the whole team, together, in the paradigm of unity.

You might boil this entire Chapter down to the nature of friendship. Would a friend of yours seek to push all responsibility and risk onto you, while also shifting onto you all of the effort to solve all problems and answer all questions? Of course not. (If you said yes, you need to reevaluate your friendships.) A friend is there to help you shoulder responsibilities, risks and effort. Friends work together to maximize the outcomes for all. Sure, friends might have different levels of experience and bring different levels of skill and ability to the friendship, but they still operate in a way that has the best interests of all friends at heart.

An Associate who approaches a Partner in a paradigm of unity and friendship is very likely to succeed in a law firm, because such an Associate is willing to help shoulder responsibility, risk and effort as part of a unified team; such an Associate is prized by Partners as rare and extremely valuable, just as true friends are rare and extremely valuable. However, an Associate who approaches a Partner in a paradigm of division and risk allocation, one who is more concerned with foisting all responsibility, risk and effort onto the shoulders of the Partners, is very likely to fail at a law firm. Partners are naturally going to avoid working with such an Associate and such an Associate will be unable to develop meaningful mentee-mentor relationships at the law firm.

If you are unsure which paradigm you are in, you need only ask yourself whether or not you expect Partners to think for you. If you expect Partners to think for you, you are in a paradigm of division and will likely fail at your law firm. If you strive to develop solutions to problems and proactively implement such solutions whenever possible—i.e., you think for yourself and do not expect Partners to think for you—you are in a paradigm of unity and will likely succeed in your law firm. If you are unsure, because you bring questions to the Partners, which might mean you expect Partners to think for you, but might not, you need only analyze the quantity and nature of the questions you bring to the Partners. If you bring all questions to the Partners, you are likely in the paradigm of division, because you are not answering for yourself even those questions that are within your capabilities. If you bring to the Partners only those questions that are beyond your capabilities, because you think for yourself in respect of all questions within your capabilities, then you are likely in the paradigm of unity.

An easy way to implement the advice of this chapter is to ask yourself, whenever you consider reaching out to a Partner for help, "Am I expecting the Partner to think for me?" Answer yourself honestly and proceed accordingly.

35

Give as much credit to others as possible.

This is my favorite paradox: the more credit you give to others, the more credibility you create for yourself. I call it the Credit/Credibility Paradox. I call it a paradox because many people assume that if they aren't getting credit for good outcomes then their credibility is not going up. They fear they will stall as compared to the development of others unless they take credit whenever and wherever possible. They are wrong.

I attended a concert by Lyle Lovett and his Large Band and it was the perfect demonstration of the Credit/Credibility Paradox. Lyle is clearly a rare and brilliant musician, lyricist and singer. But he is also a master of the Credit/Credibility Paradox. He opens the show, does a few tunes and warms the crowd up, but then he begins to introduce his band and allows each member of his band to showcase a song they've written. In the end, 80% of the concert is led by other members of his band. It is Lyle letting others have credit for their talents, while Lyle's credibility as the maestro grows to new heights.

The person I recall as being the best at this was a law firm Chairman named Bula. I cannot recall a single instance of her taking credit, or giving herself credit, for any of the amazing things that our law firm accomplished or that had been accomplished by her. She was acutely aware that all such accomplishments required teams of people. Year after year, I watched Bula accomplish greater and greater things, and yet never once did she seek to claim credit for herself.

It was not merely abstaining from grabbing credit, even when she would have been within her rights to do so, but it was Bula's generosity in giving others credit that made her shine brighter than all others. Every time I saw her speak in front of any size group, from a handful of Partners to hundreds and hundreds of Partners, and regardless of the nature of the audience, whether in front of all employees, Clients or Partners, she was meticulous in handing out praise for accomplishments. She identified people by name and conveyed the specifics of precisely what they had done well.

Another reason it is important to give credit to others, rather than simply stay silent, is that if you do not take credit for your accomplishments and you do not give others credit for such accomplishments, there is a vacuum created. Unfortunately, whenever such a vacuum is created, inevitably some unscrupulous person will quickly take the opportunity to claim credit for the accomplishments. This happened to me more than once in my career, and I wish I could go back in time and correct this mistake. I thought that being humble meant being silent about accomplishments. I was wrong. I was inadvertently creating a vacuum for others to unfairly (dishonestly) take credit for themselves. If I could, I would go back and implement the Credit/Credibility Paradox—I would be very vocal to give others who worked on such projects with me all of the credit. This would have enhanced my credibility and prevented the injustices of certain others wrongfully claiming credit in a vacuum.

As I noted above, the Chair of my law firm grew in prestige every time she told an audience about an amazing accomplishment and then listed all of the people who deserved credit for the accomplishment, while never mentioning herself. Accomplishments were never left unclaimed, but she never claimed them for herself either. She was generous with her allocation of credit to others and her credibility never stopped growing. She was genuine in giving others credit, because she knew it takes a team to achieve a really amazing accomplishment. She handed out credit to others because they deserved it, not because she was steeped in my theories of the Credit/Credibility Paradox. I think you should do the same as Bula and for the same good reason—it's the right thing to do. Perhaps knowing that the Credit/Credibility Paradox is very real and very powerful will keep you from hesitating to do the right thing. Give others credit as often as possible and watch as your own credibility rises.

36

Your job, no matter what your title, is to make your boss's job easier.

I want to emphasize that no matter what your job title might be, your job is to make your boss's job easier. This is true of every job at every level in every industry, everywhere.

In a law firm, Associates are promoted to Partner both because the law firm believes such Associates will add financially to the bottom line of the law firm if promoted and because such Associates are viewed as a good fit with the existing Partners.[4] The nature of the Partnership, sometimes referred to as the law firm's culture, is very important to the existing Partners. If you focus your energy on making your boss's job easier, you are almost cer-

4. The concept of "fit" is being analyzed closely by most major law firms to ensure that unconscious bias is mitigated or, better yet, eliminated. I have referenced the concept of "fit" in this Chapter, because I want readers of this book to understand the reality of how promotions are determined. My sincere hope is that the concept of "fit" evolves as unconscious bias is tackled by the profession. It is safe to say that even after all biases are identified—conscious or unconscious—and even after such biases are eliminated, it will remain important to the existing Partners of a law firm that candidates for promotion to Partner will fit well with the existing Partners. To use an obvious example, a law firm with extremely high ethical standards is unlikely to promote to Partner an Associate who is widely known as a cheater and a liar.

tain to be viewed by the existing Partners as fitting well in the law firm's culture.

I am not talking about fetching coffee or running errands, although there may be times when even these tasks are appropriate. What I am really talking about is having a mindset of helpfulness. Many Junior Associates have preconceived notions of what being a lawyer will be like, thinking it consists only of a specific set of lawyering tasks. They fail to realize that being a lawyer is much more than any bundle of lawyering tasks. Lawyers owe a duty to Clients to zealously represent the interests of such Clients. How we do so will vary greatly from project to project. Just as no two people are alike, no two Clients are alike. In fact, no two projects from a single Client are alike. And as no two projects are alike, the tasks required to zealously represent your Clients' interests will not be alike from project to project. This is why any preconceived notion of a lawyer having a specific set of lawyering tasks is erroneous.

Once you realize that the bundle of tasks necessary to achieve the goals of your Clients are not predefined, but rather the universe of tasks that might improve your law firm's zealous representation of Clients is infinite, you will see that there are opportunities for you to add significant value to any project so long as you have a mindset of helpfulness. Ask yourself, "When it comes to zealous representation of a Client, what can I do to make my boss's job easier?"

In a vacuum, it may seem daunting to think that you would be able to recognize ways to make your boss's job easier. Indeed, if you do things at random hoping to make your boss's job easier, there is some risk that you accidentally make his job harder. For example, if you think it will be helpful to your boss to email a Client a detailed status update you may find out that your update fails to reflect new developments that your boss knows, and which you do not know, that are critically important to the project. Clearly, taking actions at random, even if intended to be helpful is fraught with risks. Fortunately, there are three easy ways to take actions that make your boss's job easier without such risks.

1. *Do what your boss asks.* There may be times when you are asked to do tasks and given no explanation as to how such tasks fit into the project, overall. If it is clear that your boss is too busy at the moment to explain how everything fits together (See Chapter 6 *You must understand the relative value of your time to the time of others*), you should proceed to do the tasks knowing that if your boss asked you to do such tasks, then simply doing them without objection or demand of explanation is making your boss's job easier. Obviously, do the tasks on time and at the highest quality possible.
2. *Ask your boss what you can do to help.* Your boss will appreciate your show of interest and enthusiasm if you ask him what you can do to help. All good things have a limit, however, and so when you ask what you can you do to help, you must be sure to ask in a manner that is not obsequious or disruptive.
3. *Be as smart as your educational degrees suggest you are.* You have been hired by the law firm because they believe your college taught you how to think efficiently and effectively and your law school taught you how to think analytically and methodically. Use these skills and ask yourself during each project, what can you do that will make your boss's job easier?

Of the three ways to make your boss's job easier, No. 2 and No. 3 will garner you the greatest praise; No. 1 is viewed as the very minimum effort.

Never ask how you can be helpful or spontaneously do a task hoping to be helpful if you have not completed every task already asked of you. Upon completing all tasks asked of you, then consider additional ways to make your boss's life easier. The flurry of activity occupying a Partner's mind leaves little room for them to constantly be thinking of what you should do next on a project. If you think strategically and make suggestions of what you might do next on a project, your boss will be grateful. If you independently consider the skills you have, you can remind your boss as and when any such skill might be helpful in a project.

Never assume your boss knows all of your skills. You might be a wiz with graphic design and may be able to help preparing persuasive exhibits for a trial. You might have a degree in chemistry that might make you well-suited for constructing interrogatories in a drug patent case. You might love to proof read, in which case you could suggest that you review whatever document your boss is preparing before it is filed with a court or goes to a Client. The examples are numerous.

Do not fret that you will not know when or how to make your boss's job easier, because the specific context of each project will guide you. Every project for every Client will have a unique set of facts and circumstances that, when analyzed, expose a unique set of tasks required to zealously represent the Client's interests. Every project will have new ways for you to make your boss's job easier.

One specific example of an Associate making my job easier was in the context of a complicated investment reorganization. Our Client wanted to change the structure of a large investment Partnership that focused on acquiring infrastructure assets. The investment Partnership documents were several hundred pages long. The number of changes the Client wanted to negotiate with the counterparty (i.e., the other Partner in the investment Partnership) was significant. A young Associate suggested that she prepare a chart so that we could track each topic that was to be negotiated. She suggested, wisely, that we list in one column all the provisions that might be changed, put into another column what each provision currently provided, put into another column the change our Client was seeking for such provision and have a final column in which we would add notes about the status of the negotiations. I agreed and she went off and prepared the chart. It was an enormously useful document—the Associate made my job easier, very much easier. We developed the chart originally just to be a tool for us to use internally, but it wasn't long before the Client wanted a copy of our chart and it thereafter became a tool for our side's entire working group on the project. It turns out that the Associate had made many people's jobs easier.

37

Be professional, always and everywhere.

I was stunned during my career at the obliviousness of many lawyers to the fact that they are in a special role vis-à-vis their Clients and the world at large. Being a lawyer is not just a job. It is not even just a career. Being a lawyer is taking a prominent role in the framework of a society operating by the rule of law. Each lawyer in any particular moment is simultaneously a person zealously representing the interests of a Client and demonstrating to all in society how the mechanics of our civilization work in practice.

It is because of the latter aspect of this role that society holds lawyers to a very high standard of behavior and ethics. Take, for example, *pro bono*. What professions are expected to provide their services *pro bono*? To my knowledge only medicine and law. And as between medicine and law, which is so important to the proper functioning of our society that it is elevated to a Constitutional right? Yes, indeed, law—the right to an attorney if charged with a crime. Good luck finding anything in the Constitution that gives you a right to a doctor if you become ill. And what other careers or jobs are expected to provide services *pro bono*? Have you heard of a plumber, electrician, waiter, carpenter, or any other occupation (other than medicine and law) being expected to give their services freely to those who cannot afford them otherwise? This is because lawyers are the liaisons between our society's rule-of-law framework and the citizens who live in such framework. We as lawyers have a special role in our society.

Given our special role in society, it is important that lawyers always be professional. Not just in our dealings with Clients. Not just in our dealings with opposing counsel. Not just when we are in court. Not just when we are in the office. But rather always and everywhere.

There are six situations in which I see lawyers forget the importance of their role in society and forget the importance of being professional, always and everywhere.

Emails and Phone Calls

The complexities of the evolution of society are far beyond the scope of this book, but I think we can all agree that the nature of communication in our society has become less formal over the generations, just as the means of communications have grown more varied. It is imperative that lawyers not descend with the masses, but rather resist the trend of entropic communications. I fear someday the words "like" and "dude" will be all that remain of the English language.

Your Clients are paying you to be a lawyer, which for many means a master orator and writer. They have hired you because of your education and experience. They have hired you, a lawyer, to be the pillar of strength they need in a troubled or challenging time. There is a reason courthouses are designed as they are, to project stability and strength. There is a reason the United States Supreme Court building has enormous columns and architecture dating back to ancient Greece reflecting the highest quality of pure logic. Such buildings convey that law is eternal, strong and consistent regardless of the vicissitudes of fad and fashion. Clients want their lawyer to be a direct reflection of such buildings, they want to know that their lawyer is of the highest quality and personifies the nature of law itself. This is what I mean by being professional—be of your profession. Be as if you were cut from the granite pillars in Washington, D.C. Speak as though words flow from you with the perspicuity of Supreme Court Opinions. Write as though you hold the divinely-inspired quills of Thomas Jefferson or James Madison. This is the surest path to your Clients' approbation: always be professional; always be the lawyer they, and all of society, expect you to be.

It is in your best interest to be the consummate lawyer in all of your communications with your Clients. In every email and on every phone call, you should be presenting yourself as the consummate lawyer. If they view you as the consummate lawyer, you benefit from a kind of favorable prejudice they have in your work product and deference to your advice. If they begin to question your status as the consummate lawyer, you will lose such benefit and in fact you will suffer from a constant second-guessing of your work product and advice. It does not take much to undermine your Clients' views of you as the consummate lawyer. My advice is that in every email and on every phone call, always, you should be the consummate lawyer, because you are their lawyer.

With respect to emails, specifically, you should construct them with the same care you would construct a legal memorandum or brief. Even a short email should be clear, concise and formal. Write every email as though it will be shared with others, because nearly every email is shared with others. This is true whether the email is to a Client, an opposing party, a court or even your colleagues. I learned the hard way that emails I prepared as a Junior Associate were forwarded in many different situations that I did not anticipate. Once, a Partner I worked for asked me to analyze an issue and send him an email with my thoughts on the issue, which I did. I had worked for this Partner for several years and we were on friendly terms. I wrote my thoughts hastily and I assumed that he would review it and we would discuss the substantive aspects of my conclusions before providing advice to the Client. I assumed wrong. He simply forwarded my email to the Client as our firm's advice. I immediately regretted the casual approach I had used in the email; after all, the email was a reflection of me as a lawyer.

With respect to phone calls, specifically, you should refrain from slang and never speak with any artificial affectation, such as vocal fry. My hope is that by the time this book is published vocal fry will be a long-gone fad. Unfortunately, as I write this book, vocal fry seems to only be on the rise. Vocal fry is the purposeful affectation of one's voice to sound raspy, and it connotes indifference, social condescension and inexperience. It tells the listener that you are indifferent to the topic being discussed; it tells the listener that you are of high social status and are using the least effort of breath possible to even bother communicating; it tells the listener that you are inexperienced because any lawyer with experience would know that their Client does not want a lawyer who is indifferent to their situation and considers herself superior in social status to the Client.

I had the unfortunate experience of leading a conference call on which I had asked two Junior Associates to take the lead on two different topics during the course of the call. On this call there were several individuals from our Client corporation, several from the opposing party, two of the opposing party's lawyers and the three of us (me and my two Associates). As such, it was a robust telephonic gathering of about 10 to 12 people.

I assigned each of my Associates one finite topic to cover and thought doing so would give them a good opportunity to begin to become comfortable speaking on such conference calls. To be sure, such calls are very intimidating early in one's career and in fact never become entirely unintimidating.

Both of my Associates had prepared sufficiently to cover the substance of their topic with aplomb. But, to my dismay, each of my Associates used a style of communication that undermined the substantial legal research and analysis otherwise evident in their presentations. The young male Associate used the word "dude" several times as a reference to one of the individuals involved in the matter—"dude" has no place on a professional call—and the young female Associate imbued her voice with a sing-song cadence and heavy vocal fry making it impossible to take her seriously—did someone invite their child to speak on this call? It felt more like elementary school show-and-tell than a serious conference call to discuss complex legal issues.

After they had finished speaking, I restated the entirety of their presentations in a professional, lawyerly manner and the call went on from there without too much damage done. After the call, I met with them and had the unpleasant but very necessary task of explaining exactly how they had each completely undermined their own good work.

I perceived that they had spoken the way they did out of a reflex to revert to more youthful speech in a subconscious plea for leniency from the august and severe participants on the call; as if using the word "dude" or using the vocal intonations of a pre-teen would illicit sympathy from the other participants on the call. I made it very clear that nobody on the call had any inclination toward sympathy and that all they managed to do with their style of communication is render their points moot and themselves irrelevant to the conversation. I explained that if I had not been on the call to elevate the nature of the communications to professional lawyering, the Client would have been furious at the manner of our representation. I remember seeing a look of surprise when I reminded the two young Associates that they are lawyers and they better start acting like it or they won't be lawyers for long.

Video Conferences

During the COVID-19 pandemic, the use of videoconference technology increased dramatically. My hope is that by the time this book is available to the public, the COVID-19 pandemic will be an historical anomaly. I suspect, however, that even after COVID-19, videoconference technology will remain an important part of the practice of law.

My friend, Macondray, shared with me an experience he had in which he failed to present himself as professionally on a videoconference as he should have done. He had good reason, or so he thought, because the videoconference had been set up by his partner, JP.

JP was notorious for bait-and-switch tactics when it came to Client introductions. One such tactic was to set up a conference call, invite a Client and a firm partner, and then not show up himself. You can imagine how awkward, and sometimes humorous, it was for two total strangers to introduce themselves and try to determine on their own why it was that they were even on the call together. This was not the only way in which JP would bait-and-switch his partners. Sometimes the switch was the topic of the call, sometimes it was the parties joining the call, sometimes it was the deliverables expected from participants on the call. JP did this so frequently that it came to be known among the partners as being "JP'd."

So, when JP reached out to my friend Macondray to set up a videoconference, Macondray assumed it would be another bait-and-switch of some kind. Macondray made no effort to prepare, either in respect of the substance of the videoconference or his attire for the videoconference; Macondray wore a t-shirt and didn't shave. As far as Macondray was concerned, he believed he was being JP'd.

Much to Macondray's surprise, JP attended the videoconference to make a proper introduction of the Client. Also surprising to Macondray was that the potential Client had a genuine need for Macondray's legal services.

Because Macondray had not prepared for the videoconference, it went poorly. The potential Client was disappointed with the obvious lack of preparation and surprised at the overly casual appearance. In hindsight, it is clear that Macondray should have declined the invitation to the videoconference, if he believed he was being JP'd, or Macondray should have prepared properly for the videoconference.

Social Events

There is no social situation attended by your law firm colleagues, your Clients or potential Clients that is not a professional event requiring you to be professional in your behavior and communications. It's a simple rule, easy to follow, and yet many people make the mistake of dropping their lawyerly discipline in social situations.

Note the "or" in my statement, above. It is intentional. My advice is to retain your professional demeanor at any social event attended by your law firm colleagues, your Clients *or* potential Clients. Even if it is just grabbing a drink with your law firm colleagues, it is still a professional event and you are well-advised to be just as professional as if your Clients were there. Really? Why?

The reason is that throughout your career your colleagues will have innumerable opportunities to invite you to events that will include potential Clients and innumerable opportunities to refer Clients to you. Ask yourself if your colleagues are more likely or less like to do so if you have behaved foolishly or unprofessionally at events where they saw you? Will they remind themselves that the event was solely among law firm colleagues or will they be very protective of their own reputations? When colleagues invite you to events or refer Clients to you, they are joining their reputation yours. It is likely that if you acted foolishly in one setting, they will remember your behavior and feel somewhat guarded about inviting you to events to which Clients will be invited. For the same reason, it is likely they will be somewhat guarded about referring Clients to you.

Some unfortunate souls get off on the wrong foot before their careers have really started. Every summer, law firms around the world hire so-called "Summer Associates" to work for two or three months between the second and third year of law school. In the United States, the Summer Program, as it is usually called, has evolved into a kind of matchmaking ceremony whereby law firms select students they may wish to hire and law students select law firms they may wish to join and then they spend a summer together to see if there is a good fit. In truth, the vast majority of all Summer Associates are offered permanent positions at the law firms where they participate in Summer Programs. But there is always a small portion who blow it and I would estimate that 90% of those who blow it do so by nothing more than a failure to always be professional. It can happen in the blink of an eye, whether at a lunch, a dinner, a cocktail reception, a sporting event or anywhere else for that matter. A momentary lapse in judgment; a flash of immaturity; an unrestrained rambunctiousness; the stories of such moments are legendary.

Looking across all law firms in America, there were summers in which Summer Associates made sexual advances on the wives of Partners. There were summers in which Summer Associates broke into fist fights at cocktail receptions. Many times, Summer Associates became so intoxicated they vomited in front of Partners, in public places no less. Sometimes the failings were not as dramatic, but equally fatal to careers, such as summers in which Summer Associates debated Senior Partners on matters of law and refused to defer to the experience of the Senior Partners. Or summers in which summer Associates became so comfortable in the unique circumstances of being (i) very likely to receive a job offer and (ii) asked to do very little substantive work all summer that they simply stopped showing up at the office altogether or, if they did show up, they were wearing shorts and flipflops. These things all have happened at law firms. In fact, many more stories abound related to Summer Associates blowing it during their Summer Programs. It is hard to know why, and surely psychology is at play, but whatever the reasons there is always some small portion of the Summer Program participants throughout the country that sabotage their careers before they even start.

Social Media

At some point prior to applying to law schools you should clean up all of your social media accounts. Increasingly, law schools and law firms are vetting candidates by trolling their social media accounts. Once you decide to become a lawyer, you must accept the fact that your social media accounts convey to the world who you really are. And, once you decide to become a lawyer, who you really are should align with society's expectations of the consummate lawyer. If this seems unfair or inappropriate, you might want to consider a different career. It is wise to make sure whatever career you choose aligns with who you really are. Checking of social media accounts by law firms is now the normal course of action before making job offers to Summer Associates at the end of the Summer Programs. If your social media shows you engaged in embarrassing, immature or downright inappropriate activities, you can rest assured that you will not be given an offer to join the law firm.

Public At Large & Road Rage

My advice to always be professional extends to your existence out in public, generally. This is because you never know who might be a potential Client, who might be employed by a current Client, who might simply have influence in your community, or who might even be someone from your own law firm.

This crystalized for me after hearing the story of a friend of mine, Ted. Ted was an Associate with me in 2005. Ted had been working very long hours, starting before sunrise and going well into the night, for days. One evening, during this hectic period for Ted, our firm was hosting a social event for Clients in a ballroom at a hotel that was a good thirty minutes' drive from our offices. Ted pulled himself away from his work, knowing that he needed to make an appearance at the social event, and started his drive to the ballroom. The onramp to the freeway near our offices merged from two lanes into one lane and for no good reason, the car behind Ted accelerated and whipped around in front of him to have access to the freeway ahead of him. The car that cut around Ted was a brand-new M series BMW, which at the time was as cool of a sports car as anyone could ever want. Ted was outraged, thinking, "what kind of a jerk needs to show off a fancy sports car by cutting other people off on the freeway onramp?" Ted spent the next thirty minutes playing chase on the freeway trying to catch up to the BMW and give the driver a piece of his mind. It was obvious the BMW driver was taunting him. Ted would get close to catching up and then the BMW would speed away. Ted shouted from inside his car and gesticulated wildly. Over and again, Ted would accelerate to catch up, planning at least to show the driver some offensive sign language, but the BMW would accelerate, switch lanes abruptly, and so on. Ted grew angrier and angrier. Ted was so angry, he thought about ignoring his own destination and following the BMW, but he was unsure exactly what he might do if he caught the BMW. It turned out that following the BMW wasn't necessary, because it exited the freeway at the same exit Ted was to take for our firm's event that evening. Then the BMW made the same series of turns Ted needed to make and ultimately pulled into the parking lot of the same hotel where our firm's event was being held. As they parked, Ted saw that it was the Senior Partner of his practice area getting out of the BMW. Suddenly, rather than wishing he had the opportunity to place his middle finger squarely in the BMW driver's face, Ted was racing through his mind to determine if the BMW driver at any point could have seen any of Ted's silent screams or gestures. Ted was awash with concern that his temper tantrum had been noticed; he was both personally embarrassed and professionally alarmed. Thankfully, the Senior Partner knew it was Ted all along and had not noticed anything that suggested Ted was angry. In fact, the Senior Partner thought he and Ted had been playing together on the drive. The Senior Partner got out of his car smiling and approached Ted with a kind of youthful gusto and said, pointing at his car, "What do you think? I just bought her last week. Isn't she beautiful!"

Rough Drafts

There is no such thing as a rough draft if you share it with others. Every draft you ever show anybody of any of your work is the final draft as far as they are concerned. Always be professional. Always provide to others the most professional draft you can prepare. This advice will save you unnecessary embarrassment, frustration and potentially harsh consequences.

I cannot recall the number of times a Client, eager to gain forward momentum on a project, asked that I share a rough draft of a legal memorandum, contract or other germane document. It was always the same. They would say, quite convincingly, that they knew I was still working on the document and knew it would not be in its final shape, but could I possibly share a rough draft so they could get started on their part of the project? I fell for this, once.

I sent a very rough draft legal memorandum to a Client who had convinced me that I was not to worry, he just wanted to see where the analysis was heading and perhaps use the draft to begin formulating his own thoughts on the project. I sent the draft and, sadly, the Client proceeded to share my draft with others at his company and before I knew what was happening, I was on a conference call with a half dozen people being peppered with questions and concerns they had with my memorandum. I said several times that I had shared the rough draft under the impression it was to be used informally by one person—and I felt bad doing this as I called him out—but it didn't matter. The readers of the memorandum were not in a frame of mind to differentiate between rough draft and final version when it came to a memorandum from their high-priced lawyer. It was a painful conference call and it made finishing the memorandum even more painful. Not only did I need to finish it on a much faster timeline, to correct the record in terms of advice I was deemed to have provided, but I also had to suffer subsequent conference calls in which, on the one hand, some participants noted that they were glad their input had improved the memorandum (input that was entirely unnecessary because the only reason the improvements were not in the memorandum they originally saw was I had been foolish enough to send a rough draft) and, on the other hand, some participants challenged me on why I had changed my advice on various points (which was not advice I was changing but rather advice I had never completed in the rough draft of the memorandum). I think it was at least two weeks of phone calls and emails before everything was straightened out—all because I chose in a moment of gullibility to deviate from always being professional. If I had retained my consummate lawyer mentality, I would have insisted upon being professional and as such insisted upon not sending a rough draft to the Client until it sufficiently reflected the quality of my legal research and writing as a professional.

It was a tedious and painful lesson, but it taught me that there is no such thing as a rough draft if you share it with others. Any work you share with others should reflect the best of your abilities. Doing otherwise is a failure to be professional. My lesson learned reinforced my belief that it is important to be professional, always and everywhere.

38

Think like the Client.

There are two ways in which thinking like the Client will help you succeed. First, thinking like the Client will enable you to apply the Lawyer's Golden Rule—do for your Client what you would want done for you if you were the Client. Second, thinking like a Client will keep you from alienating your Client by thinking like a lawyer and erroneously expecting the Client to think like a lawyer.

The Lawyer's Golden Rule

Do for your Client what you would want done for you if you were the Client. This simple rule will always steer you right—it will help you align your services with the expectations of the Client, which is important if you want to have a happy Client who will bring you more work and refer other Clients to you.

Many times, I would simply state some version of this rule when an Associate had a question about how to proceed on a matter. If there is more than one way to accomplish a task, use the approach you would want your lawyer to use if you were the Client. If there are competing requests from a Client and you are not sure which to do first, then you need only do first that which you would want done first if you were the Client. When you are extremely tired, overwhelmed with work and, yet, realize that with another hour of effort you could confirm a legal point that you are pretty sure you know but aren't 100% sure, do what you would want your lawyer to do if you were the Client (usually, the answer is that you should work the extra hour). In many, many situations the questions you will face during your career can be answered simply by asking, "What would the Client want?"

Your Client is Not (Always) a Lawyer

What I am about to show you is a major distinction between a seasoned lawyer and an inexperienced lawyer. A typical inexperienced lawyer has the following commonalities with other inexperienced lawyers: She performed well in high school, performed well in college, performed well in law school; and she is typically between 25 and 29 years old when she starts at a law firm as a lawyer. If we focus on a 25-year-old, then 12% of her entire life was spent in law school, and roughly 40% of her thinking years—high school, college and law school—were spent in law school. It is only natural that such a person would have limited insight into how the rest of the world thinks and where the rest of the world focuses their time and energy. Spoiler alert: the rest of the world doesn't think like lawyers and they aren't focused on lawyering.

I tell you this because of the frequency with which inexperienced lawyers blow it with their Clients, even after having done excellent legal work. I will use an example from securities law and show you two different outcomes, based entirely on (i) whether or not the lawyer keeps in mind that the Client is not a lawyer, and (ii) whether or not the lawyer thinks like the Client.

The premise for the scenario is that the Client holds shares he acquired in his capacity as a director of a private company and wants to sell those shares to his neighbor. The Client has asked,

"Am I permitted to sell the shares?" A Partner has confidence in a particular Associate and instructs the Associate to research the question and get back to the Client directly, and come back to the Partner only if the Associate has questions. Let's assume the Associate has done excellent legal research and knows exactly what the law requires when it comes to selling shares of a private company, but a definitive answer to the Client's question cannot be given without knowing three additional facts. 1. Is the Client still a director of the private company? 2. How long has the Client held the shares since receiving them from the private company? 3. Are there any agreements between the Client and the private company or between the Client and other shareholders that might have implications for selling the shares?

An inexperienced lawyer will often write a lengthy email to the Client explaining the securities laws related to the sale of shares in a company. In this case, there is a special subset of rules for selling shares of a private company. These rules differ for company insiders, such as Directors, versus others who might own shares in the private company. Specifically, there are certain holding periods that might be relevant. The Associate includes all of this in his email, going on and on, perfectly setting forth the body of law that will enable the Client to answer the Client's question. The wayward Associate is essentially under the misconception that his or her job is to summarize the law for the Client and then let the Client make a conclusion.

A seasoned lawyer would, instead, send a very short email to the Client: "I have concluded my research, but have three short questions before being able to provide definitive advice. Are you still a director, officer or employee at the company? When did you receive the shares you want to sell to your neighbor? Did you sign any agreements, such as a Shareholders Agreement, Employment Agreement, Founders Agreement or the like that might have additional rules for selling your shares?"

You might think, "but Paul, the first approach would enable the Client to make his own conclusion. Isn't that what the Client would want?" No. The Client is not a lawyer. Sending him a treatise on securities law is definitely not what the Client wants. If he wanted to analyze law and make a conclusion, he would not have hired a lawyer in the first place. The inexperienced lawyer's approach will annoy the Client, because the natural reaction for the Client will be to try and digest the lengthy legal advice and make the conclusion. That will be frustrating for a non-lawyer. Some Clients will immediately recognize the approach as erroneous and simply reply, "all I want is for you to tell me the answer," at which point you are right where the seasoned lawyer's approach started—i.e., you need to ask the three questions. But unlike the seasoned lawyer, the inexperienced Associate has annoyed the Client and caused undue delay.

The approach of the seasoned lawyer will lead to a smooth conclusion for the Client. The Client will answer three easy questions of fact he would know off the top of his head. From those answers, the seasoned lawyer will be able to complete the legal analysis and provide a clear yes or no answer to the Client's question.

Clients love yes or no answers and all other forms of clear advice. They dislike "it depends" even though in law, it often does depend on the specific facts. To bridge the gap between the Clients' preference for short, clear answers and the need to be precise when providing legal advice, I would often provide the short answer up front in a standalone paragraph and then follow it with some considerations, in layman's terms, for the Client to keep in mind that could change the outcome of the legal advice.

There are times when your Client will be a lawyer, such as internal counsel at a company that is your Client. It might surprise you to learn that even Clients who are lawyers are not interested in being lawyers in respect of the issues they send to you as their outside counsel. Internal counsel at a company is more likely to ask you to share a written form of your legal analyses and conclusions—i.e., a traditional legal memorandum—than Clients who are not lawyers, but this is precisely because they do not want to do the legal work themselves (or they wouldn't have hired you). As such, even if your Client is a lawyer, it is risky to assume that what they want from you is a regurgitation of the law. They will likely want a clear yes or no answer from you, just as a non-lawyer Client will.

It all comes down to thinking like your Client.

The above analysis focuses on the specific mistake commonly made by inexperienced lawyers—i.e., sending advice written in a way that only other lawyers would be able to decipher. It is merely one example, however, of the many ways lawyers fail to follow the guiding principle—think like your Client. The example should not supersede the rule. Each Client is different and you will learn each Client's way of thinking if you pay attention. If, contrary to the example above, a non-lawyer-Client wants to be tutored on the law itself, that's great. You can do that easily. If a lawyer-Client wants a simple yes or no answer, that's also great. You need not inundate him with all of the law behind the answer. Ditto for a non-lawyer-Client that does not want to hear the legal mumbo jumbo or a lawyer-Client that loves to hear all the legal mumbo jumbo. It is all about providing legal service tailored to each particular Client. The only way to tailor your legal services appropriately is to know how each Client thinks and then to think like the Client as you provide your legal services to each such Client.

39

The author's professional background.

I graduated from The Law School at the University of Virginia in 1998. Prior to law school, I was a financial program specialist in the International Funds Branch within the U.S. Department of the Treasury in Washington, D.C. Following graduation from Law School, I became a member of the bar in both California and New York. During my early career at Linklaters in London and then Pillsbury in San Francisco, I represented companies and investment banks in Initial Public Offerings (IPOs), both in respect of stock offerings and bond offerings; and I represented companies in mergers and acquisitions, both in respect of private and public companies. Upon joining Morgan Lewis in 2005, I represented companies sponsoring or investing in venture capital funds and private equity funds. My practice was most distinguished, however, by my representation of world-leading private foundations and public charities in connection with novel investment structures and activities focused on global social impact, primarily in medicine, education and agriculture. Such social impact clients have included, among others, the Bill and Melinda Gates Foundation, the Humane Society of the United States, the Lumina Foundation for Education, the National Geographic Society, the Walmart Foundation, Omidyar Network (ON Foundation), Soros Economic Development Fund, the Ford Foundation, and University Hospitals Health System.

I was promoted to partner at Morgan Lewis in 2008 and I was an active member of the hiring committee for nearly a decade. From 2014 through 2019, I was the global leader of the Private Equity Funds practice area at Morgan Lewis. My responsibilities covered partners and associates in offices around the world, including Boston, Dallas, Dubai, Hong Kong, London, Miami, New York, San Francisco, Silicon Valley, Singapore, Tokyo and Washington D.C.

I have been recognized as a "rising star" in California by *Super Lawyers*, recommended nationally by *The US Legal 500*, and ranked globally and nationally by *Chambers Global* and *Chambers USA*, respectively. I was part of a six-partner leadership team for Morgan Lewis's Asset Management Practice Group when it was awarded the *Asset Management Practice Group of the Year* by *Law360*. I was a member of the American College of Investment Counsel and the National Association of Public Pension Attorneys.

My wife, MaryKay, and I now live in the Lake Tahoe area of California. Although I retired from Morgan Lewis, I still practice law for one client, because such client is revolutionizing the way in which money is raised and allocated to early-stage medical discoveries; I simply cannot decline the opportunity to do my part in changing the world for the better.

Made in the USA
Las Vegas, NV
15 September 2024

95301594R00128